KEYS TO KINGDOM AUTHORITY SERIES

LIVING A LIFESTYLE OF FASTING:
BREAKING THROUGH TO THE BEST YOU

BISHOP DARRYL F. HUSBAND SR. D.MIN.

**LIVING A LIFESTYLE OF FASTING:
BREAKING THROUGH TO THE BEST YOU**

©2009 Life More Abundant Ministries

Published by LuLu.com

Printed in the United States of America
All rights reserved. No part of this publication may be reproduced, stored in a retrieval system or transmitted in any form or by any means- electronic, mechanical, photocopy, recording or any other- without the prior written permission of the publisher. The only exception is brief quotations in printed reviews.

Unless otherwise noted; Holy Bible, New International Version®. Copyright © 1973, 1978, 1984 International Bible Society. Used by permission of Zondervan. All rights reserved.

Scripture taken from the Amplified® Bible,
Copyright © 1954, 1958, 1962, 1964, 1965, 1987 by The Lockman Foundation Used by permission." (www.Lockman.org)

Scripture quotations identified as KJV are from the King James Version of the Bible.

Scripture taken from The Message. Copyright ©1993, 1994, 1995, 1996, 2000, 2001, 2002. Used by permission of NavPress Publishing Group."

Scripture taken from the New American Standard Bible®, Copyright © 1960,1962,1963,1968,1971,1972,1973,1975,1977,1995 by The Lockman Foundation. Used by permission." (www.Lockman.org)

Credits
Typist: Joy Blathers
Copy Editor: Sandra Johnson
Cover Design: Larry Cozart and Hugh Jones

ISBN: 978-0-557-24490-4

Dedication

I dedicate this book to the almighty God who saw my life spinning in a whirlwind of indiscipline, which threatened my ability to fully actualize my potential. He thought enough of me to speak to me about changing the course of my destiny. I will undoubtedly be eternally grateful and the kingdom of darkness will suffer innumerable losses because of my rescue.

To Eric, Jason, Daytriel, Darryl II and Gabriella, and every son and daughter in the faith, I dedicate this book to you as you pursue Him in all you say and do. May you find the joy of the Lord faster because of laboring before Him.

Acknowledgements

I want to acknowledge my lovely bride who always allows me time with God to release the gifts in me to bless others. I thank her for giving me wonderful children who will be kingdom blessings to the nations. I write so that they too may read and use as weapons to destroy every stronghold the enemy has set up in and out of the Body of Christ.

My Spiritual daughters Joy and Sandra, I have written nothing that you didn't have your hands in. You are both jewels of which there is no way to place a value.

A big thank you to Ralph and Susan McIntosh, you are very special to me. Susan, I thank you especially for your testimony contribution to this work.

Bishop Wellington Boone, I love you man of God. Your friendship and confidence in me to represent your organization as one of your Bishops, still humbles me.

Bishop William Murphy Jr. thanks for including me in on the plan to help the church return to the house of prayer.

Table of Contents

Dedication ii

Acknowledgements iii

Foreword vi

1 Preparation for the Power Zone 1

2 The Goal of the Christian Life and the Key That Unlocks the Door 12

3 Types of Fasts: Designing the Fast for Your Need 37

4 Starving the Flesh 51

5 Eat All You Can- Building Up the Spirit Man 72

6 Breaking Strongholds and Canceling Generational Curses 90

7 Canceling Generational Curses and Breaking Strongholds Part II: The Bridge to the Future 102

8 Fasting: The Key to Revelation for the Vision Impaired 116

9 Fasting As a Sabbath- Your Body Needs Rest-oration 127

10 For Tradition or Triumph: Lent or Life-Style 139

11 Kingdom Consciousness: My New Beginning 150

12 When I am Fasting, What About My Children? 165

13 Testimony from a Saint: Shut up Stomach! Hello God! 177

Addendum: What a Christian Looks Like 186

Bibliography 187

About The Author 190

Foreword

I remember one day a few years ago when I walked into Bishop Husband's office and saw on the floor the books and the space where it was obvious he had been calling on the Lord as he was praying and fasting for some weeks. I felt that there was such an anointing that I didn't even want to walk there. I know that this book is not only important for its written content but also because the person who has written it has lived what is written. Jesus said, "Believe me that I am in the Father, and the Father in me: or else believe me for the very works' sake" (John 14:11). He was saying in effect that My works match My words. I can say that in this book by Bishop Husband on fasting that his works match his words. I believe that there will be a release of power if you read it and take it in and do it. God bless you.

At His feet with you,
Bishop Wellington Boone

1
Preparation for the Power Zone

> *"Fasting possesses great power. If practiced with the right intention, it makes one a friend of God. The demons are aware of that."*
> Quintus Tertullian (160-220 A.D.; Christian Ecclesiastical author,)

Years ago, one of my sons in ministry stood before our congregation to deliver a sermon. He had come to Christ after attending a thirty day revival. He laid down the weapons of his warfare (literally speaking) and humbly prepared himself for ministry. The night of his sermon was one I was impatient to experience. I waited to see this young man who the streets knew as a feared fighter who was never to be taken lightly by an opponent. The night arrived and the moment came. He stood to offer his message. Then after about 10 minutes, he was done. After the message, I took him in my office and offered to him my very poignant evaluation of his message to us. His topic that night was, "Powerless Disciples". As loving as I could, but with the intent to inspire him to attain what I saw in him, I said these words, "Son, tonight you were the epitome of a powerless disciple."

I know you are saying to yourself, "What a cold, biting, world shaking potentially ministry breaking, evaluating remark." And you may be correct, but every father must know his children. I spoke the truth in love and today that same powerless disciple is as focused a minister as has ever come out of our ministry. He has seen people healed time and time again in Sunday and Wednesday services and has yet to come back to his home church without a life changing message.

The evaluation I shared with him is not uncommon behavior or would it be an unfair analysis of much of the church world today. A large percentage of the church world operates in a "taker" mentality. Far too often, the question is, what can I get out of the church? They never ask what I have to offer of myself. How can I be prepared for the service of the kingdom, is the furthest question from their minds. No wonder many of our churches have electricity with no light, and air conditioning or heat, with no power. God said this to Jeremiah,

> "A horrible and shocking thing has happened in the land. The prophets prophesy lies, the priests rule by their own authority, and my people love it this way. But what will you do in the end?"(Jeremiah 5:30-31)

In the end, we must give an account for our influences. Every *gift* (we are gifts from God), will have to give an account. Every person who was given a gift, as well as every ministry in the body of Christ, will have their day in the *real* Supreme Court. Power is not the problem. People who God has chosen are offered the resources to change the world, yet have not tapped into them. God has given us everything that pertains to life and Godliness.

I Peter 1:13-22 says, "*¹³Therefore, prepare your minds for action; be self-controlled; set your hope fully on the grace to be given you when Jesus Christ is revealed. ¹⁴As obedient children, do not conform to the evil desires you had when you lived in ignorance. ¹⁵But just as he who called you is holy, so be holy in all you do; ¹⁶for it is written: "Be holy, because I am holy."*

> *¹⁷Since you call on a Father who judges each man's work impartially, live your lives as strangers here in reverent fear. ¹⁸For you know that it was not with perishable things such as silver or gold that you were redeemed from the empty way of life handed down to you from your forefathers, ¹⁹but with the precious blood of Christ, a lamb without blemish or defect. ²⁰He was chosen before the creation of the world, but was revealed in these last times for your sake.*
>
> *²¹Through him you believe in God, who raised him from the dead and glorified him, and so your faith and hope are in God. ²²Now that you have purified yourselves by obeying the truth so that you have sincere love for your brothers, love one another deeply, from the heart. ²³For you have been born again, not of perishable seed, but of imperishable, through the living and enduring word of God."*

He is our power source. His power in us results in radical transformation wherever we choose to take it. Our objective in this book is to walk with you on a journey to the center of the will of God. It will require an initial evaluation, a little honesty, desire, discipline, and a lot of patience.

The Evaluation

The New Testament is truly our snapshot of the image of God that we were created to be. We are awesomely and pleasantly surprised (even though foretold), with a personal appearance by God. The revelation we get from the Hebrew writer says this about Jesus, *"The son is the radiance of God's glory and the exact representation of his being..."* Hebrews 1:3 NIV. Truly, when you see Him, you've seen *the* Father. Each account of Jesus, from the synoptic depiction of the first three gospels, which begins with the miracles of his birth, to the amazing insight of John to take us beyond the earthly to the eternal origin, we see God's love for us. This is His story. Yet, it could also be labeled, the introduction to the disciples' story. It is a training manual for world leadership. It is a testing ground for every disciple to measure themselves by, to see whether they be in the faith or not. Every person who says "Lord, Lord" is not kingdom material. *Saying* Lord is not the prerequisite for a crown; it is believing that really matters.

Believing is confirmed by the power of demonstration. There is a distinct difference between preaching the gospel and living or doing the gospel. The litmus test or evaluation for every believer can be easily drawn from statements Jesus made to those He chose. Yes, there were requirements Jesus had of those He chose. Are you one of the chosen? If not yet, then choose to be chosen, and keep reading till you get a revelation of what that means. It is adoption into what is called, "sonship." That has nothing to do with gender, but everything to do with a relationship and an inner resemblance of the Father. Here are some questions for you as a chosen one.

Question #1
Who do you say I am?

Question #2
Are you keeping my commandments?

Question #3
Are you going into the world where you are, to preach, teach, make disciples for them to observe everything the Lord has commanded you?

Question #4
Do you lay your hands on the sick so they can recover?

Question #5
Do you pray daily and often (without ceasing, which means talking and listening to the Father)?

Question #6
Do you fast? How often?

Question #7
Have you ever asked the Father what He was not pleased with in your life and then quit after He showed you? Ever asked Him to show you completely what His will is for you life?

Honesty

In one of the Bible Study nights in our church, we did an exercise. I asked every person to do the same thing I am proposing to you now. Take out a piece of paper (or write in the back of this book on the page provided under the addendum section: What a Christian Looks Like) and take 3 minutes or so and quickly write everything that comes to your mind without letting your pen pause too much. Then return to this page and continue your reading. Please, do it now. Come on, it will help you. Time yourself. Take 3 minutes.

Now that you have completed that exercise you should have a nice list. If you are a Christian, you may have a long list. If you are not a Christian, it may be short. Whichever it is, the answers to the questions are in the greatest book the world has ever seen. It is called the Bible. Listed in the addendum are some answers I wrote, as well as others who were present that night. (See List in Addendum)

The bottom line after the exercise was this. After the exercise, my next question to them was responded to with sounds, not words. The question to them and the one I pose to you now is this; does the list you wrote down describe you? Do you look like the Christian that you described? If not, why not?

What habits do you have, that in refusing to break, you are hindering your ability to operate fully in the power of God? Proverbs 28:2 says, "The Righteous are as bold as lions." Have you ever wondered why? It is because they live like what they were made to be. Their sins are past. Satan has no recent reminders that will suffocate them shouting their triumphant testimonies loudly. Their secrets have been revealed. They have made the miseries of their past, a ministry. Satan could not shut the mouth of Mary Magdalene. Everybody knew her past. She could care less. Her past was a forgotten rubbish pile dumped on the head of the enemy. She lives freely without baggage. She never looks over her shoulder. So when the sight of a risen Savior presented itself to her, she boldly ran and told the disciples.

Here is a question that causes us to prioritize our lives. If you had 30 days left to live what would you do? What would you *quit* doing to get yourself ready for eternity? What relationships would you mend? Are there things or ways in your lifestyle you would change? Habits you would break? Are there any secret things in your life that you are not proud of, and you know God has repeatedly encouraged you to change? Is your life "Kingdom of God" ready? Can you walk out of this world into the next without having to have your spiritual baggage checked and unauthorized contraband forced to be discarded by security?

If the answer to these questions is no, then why wait to change what you are doing with your life? You may not be given a thirty day notice before checking out. Look yourself in the face and take off the mask. It is time to get ready for the supernatural life you were born to live on earth, but first let's take the honesty exam. I prefer calling it "the Peter Examination". Don't slump down in your chair. It really is like a quiz, because it has two questions that are asked three times. It is easy because the answers are given, yet it is comprehensive and heart challenging. It is short, yet it may take a lifetime for you to truly answer the questions. The examination is found in John's Gospel, chapter 21. The first question is this, "Do you love me more than these?" The second is like unto the first, "Do you love me?"

If you read the New American Standard Bible Version, you get a feel for the answer Jesus gives and is looking for. He says, "Tend to my lambs", "Shepherd my sheep", and "Tend to my sheep". Let us expound upon these questions my dear friend. Do you love Jesus more than your job, money or material things? Do you love Him more than you love your friends, family, your status, rank or position of authority? Are you discipling anyone into the family of God? Are you reproducing after the God-kind?

Question number two was simply, do you love Him? If you do, then the next answer Jesus gives us raises heart challenging questions about our place in the body of Christ. Are you leading sheep (people) in the same way I would lead them? Is anyone saying they follow you because you follow Christ? Are you covering any group of people with prayer? Are you teaching, nurturing, and casting a compelling vision to others (even if it is the one given to you by your local shepherd [pastor]. Are you mature enough to lead sheep, not just lambs? What is your faith level?

Question number three is the same as number two, yet Jesus is asking the deeper love question to Peter and us. Do you love me beyond rebuke? Do you love me even if you too have to die? Do you love me more than all the worldly desires you have? Am I more important to you than your dreams, wants and feelings? Am I Lord? Prove it! Will you spend your life making the growing up or maturing of people your priority? Will you invest your life in the kingdom, so that when you enter a room, you never leave it the same way you entered it? By this I mean, that the people who you encounter in that room will experience Christ because you have been there. Seeds are planted for a harvest of righteousness. Again, will you make feeding sheep (people) a priority? Will you help them to reproduce and replenish the earth with other people made in the image of God? That is what I call, the "Peter Examination"!

If you begin taking the exam and feeling dejected, rejected or convicted, then it is a certainty that you are a candidate for finishing this book. If the exam didn't move you in any way, you are undoubtedly a candidate for finishing this book for other reasons. Suffice it to say, that at the very least, you need to read on for explanation to help others who need to put the super into their natural, and operate in the God-kind of life they were born to live. How do they do that?

The Desire

The writer of Ecclesiastes penned these words of dictation from God, "...Also, He has set eternity in their hearts, without which man cannot find out the world God makes from the beginning even to the end." (Ecclesiastes 3:11). The Good News Bible version says it this way, "He has given us a desire to know the future..." Every person has inside of them the breath of God. It is that breath that gives us life eternally. We choose to breathe natural or supernatural air or heir. The Psalmist expressed it this way, "He satisfies the longing soul and fills the hungry soul with goodness"[2] (Psalm 107:19 KJV). Are you seeing it yet? Well let's push a little further. Why settle for mediocrity when great is available? Why settle for walking when you can fly? Why settle for living in the dark when sunshine and light is available? Why settle for carnal Christianity, wilderness' provisions, visitor's accommodations, and *some* access in the house/kingdom, when you can live and operate in "sonship"? The blessings and privileges of the son belong to you. You are a joint-heir. You are a child of the owner. You are not a tenant.

Mark 11 gives us a view of what Adam was created to live like, which clues us in on our created standard, or mode of operation. Jesus is our model. He clues us in on what we were made to look and act like (dominator). It is embarrassing to see how far we are from our prototype. Jesus came to call us back to our rightful places. It is our destiny to have dominion. Just two chapters earlier, He heals a boy possessed by a demon, and tells the disciples the key ingredient to the kind of power exercised. He shared with them that some power you can only have by prayer and fasting (Mark 9:29 {KJV} – "*^{29}And he said unto them, this kind can come forth by nothing, but by prayer and fasting.*"). We will return to that verse in later chapters of this book, but in Chapter 11 of the Gospel of Mark, Jesus speaks to a tree, that's right, He speaks to a tree. It was the second time. The first time he asked it for some fruit. The second time He spoke barrenness to that tree, because it would not give Him its fruit. He in essence said to it, that it would not produce fruit for itself anymore because it would not produce it for Him who made it. He says to the tree, "May no one ever eat fruit from you again (Mark 11:14)." The next day they all passed by the fig tree again and Peter said to Jesus, in what I am certain was a surprising tone, that the fig tree which Jesus cursed was now withered (dried up). Jesus spoke, and it happened. Death and life *are* in the power of the tongue. From the beginning of time, our words were meant to be a creative force in the universe. Elijah prayed and rain ceased. He prayed again and the elements returned.

    The question arises then, what is your desire? Do you desire to survive? Are you satisfied with merely existing, living the dominated life? Do you know your place in the heart of God? How He cherishes you and holds you as His prize creation? He intended for you to rule here, not be ruled. He is waiting for you to desire an upgrade. You were not born for any other class, but the God-class. Now let's plot the rest of the course to your designed destiny. Desire is only the beginning. The next step is discipline.

① Set Eternity in our hearts

Discipline

Discipline is defined as, "training intended to illicit a specified pattern of behavior or character."[1] Without discipline it is difficult to accomplish anything. For years I struggled with discipline. I wanted to pray, to write books and finish school, but I could not, because I was undisciplined. My time was not ordered. I did not like routines. I preferred freelancing through life. I noticed however, that I had great ideas that seldom materialized, because I lacked the discipline to work on them and carry them through.

Fasting is a discipline. Fasting requires discipline. It means that you are willing to set aside some time daily to consume the will of God through prayer and meditating on His word. It requires you to give up things you like to eat and drink, refusing them, for the purpose of being able to train your thinking, your wants and feelings, and submit them to the will of God. We will go into this further in later chapters, but suffice it to say that fasting will require of each of us to plan our day. What to do, when to do it and how. Planning our meals (physical and spiritual) is crucial. How often do we have bible intake (reading)? So that we have the right guidance *for* our day, what times do we focus completely on prayer *during* the day? The planning then must be followed as though your life depended upon it. You are a commitment away from an amazing life which breathes rare air. It can only be described for lack of better words as, "morning by morning new mercies I see". Your discipline will determine your development. Your development will decide your destination. Isn't it time to book your flight to the realm of the supernatural life? Before you burst with excitement, we have one final, yet important detail to cover.

---

[1] *Merriam-Webster Online Dictionary* Merriam-Webster, Incorporated, 2005

Patience

Enough cannot be said about the element of patience during the process of transformation. I encourage you, my dear friend and fellow pursuer of kingdom standard living, to see fasting as a life-style and not just an event. Many people who fast do not get it right after several tries. Failure then, entices them to quit trying. Never forget that anything worth having is worth trying again and again, until you get it right.

The testimony of one of my dearest members, Mother Elizabeth Cheatham, is appropriate. She is in her sixties and shared with our congregation that she finally succeeded in completing her first fast. Her honesty blessed me. Her patience blessed her. She could not have had that testimony unless she decided and desired to receive something from God, and believed she could eventually discipline herself to the point of overcoming issues she faced. That took patience. For this, I applaud her.

In the coming chapters, we will journey together to a place in Christ that will be an incredible blessing. I have one regret; that I may not be present to actually see the *you* that has been waiting to be revealed. Nevertheless, I am excited for you and if the Lord says so, I would love for you to share with me your story after you have completed the journey. Whatever you do, do not quit. The end will justify the means. The results will be worth the journey.

Next stop, we will investigate a little history about fasting, as well as the goals of the Christian life. Are you excited yet? Well I am excited enough for the both of us. There is a power filled disciple inside of you waiting to emerge. Open the door and shout, Come Out!

2
The Goal of the Christian Life and the Key That Unlocks the Door

> *"Fasting with a pure heart and motives, I have discovered, brings personal revival and adds power to our prayers. Personal revival occurs because fasting is an act of humility. Fasting gives opportunity for deeper humility as we recognize our sins, repent, receive God's forgiveness, and experience His cleansing of our soul and spirit. Fasting also demonstrates our love for God and our full confidence in His faithfulness."*
> Bill Bright (1921-2003; "The Coming Revival"; American founder of "Campus Crusade for Christ")

Thomas à Kempis said, "It is vanity to love what is passing away with all speed, and not to be hastening thither where endless joy abideth." He was born in or around 1390, educated by medieval mystics, ordained a priest in his early twenties and spent the rest of his life in a monastery focusing on the importance of the interior life, so that one could mature spiritually. Thomas Hamerken (Kempen is where he was born) understood so well about the goal of the Christian life, that it is said of his writing, *The*

Imitation of Christ, that it is "second only to the Bible in popularity among religious literature". With pinpoint accuracy he writes about in the pursuit of "the walk every Christian needs to have". Listen to one of the prayers he was praying and you will agree that his words are a penetrating force in any life that is seriously seeking God.

He says, *"O most sweet and most loving Lord, whom I now desire with all devotion to receive. Thou knowest my infirmity and the necessity which I endure; under how great evils and vices I lie prostrate; how often I am oppressed, tempted, troubled, and defiled. To Thee do I come for remedy, to Thee do I pray for consolation and relief: I speak to Him who knoweth all things, to whom my whole interior is manifest, and who alone can perfectly console and assist me. Thou knowest what good things I stand most in need of and how poor I am in virtues. Behold, I stand before Thee, poor and naked, begging grace and imploring mercy. Feed Thy hungry beggar, inflame my coldness with the fire of Thy love, and enlighten my blindness with the brightness of Thy Presence. Turn for me all earthly things into bitterness, all things grievous and adverse into patience, and all low and created things into contempt and oblivion. Raise up my heart to Thee into heaven, and suffer me not to wander upon earth. Mayest Thou alone be delightful to me henceforth and for evermore. For Thou only art my meat and drink, my love and my joy, my sweetness and my whole good. Oh, that with Thy Presence Thou wouldst totally inflame, consume, and transform me into Thyself, that I may be made one spirit with Thee by the grace of internal union, and by the melting of ardent love! Suffer me not to go from Thee hungry and dry; but deal with me in Thy Mercy, as Thou hast often dealt so wonderfully with Thy Saints. What marvel if I should be wholly set on fire by Thee, and should die to myself, since Thou art a fire always burning and never failing, a love purifying hearts and enlightening the understanding!"*[2]

Indeed we find our strength in God. The joy of the Lord is our strength. When we seek His presence, it is there where we find joy and thereby strength. Nothing else can satisfy or quench our thirst in this thing we call life. Yet, how often are we found searching for love in all the wrong places. The way to the greatest love we shall ever know is through death. Yes, the way up is down. The goal of the Christian life is to die so we can live. It is a constant marriage. Deadness brings forth life. Strange but true, death is the door to life.

Of course when we talk about death it is in the sense of killing the flesh. Destroying the very right of the feelings, desires and thinking, to operate in a ruling capacity over the spirit man, is what killing the flesh is all about. As we journey together (in the next chapter) we will see how to make that flesh man, carnal character, submit to the spirit man. It is difficult to accomplish this do this without fasting. There are ingredients involved in fasting that participate in the flesh killing process. For instance, fasting must include worship. Worship is your warfare weapon that strengthens you in your fast. Church Pierce, in his book, *The Worship Warrior*, says, "When we worship, we bow down or stoop before someone in an act of submission or reverence. Worship actually means, to make oneself low. It is the opposite of self exaltation. Therefore, to exalt the Lord actually means for us to fall at Hs feet and honor Him for who He is in our lives."[3] The truest and

---

[2] Thomas ă Kempis, *The Imitation of Christ*, Grand Rapids, MI, 1993, p 4
[3] Chuck Pierce and John Dickson, *The Worship Warrior*, Regal from Gospel Light, Ventura, CA , 2002. Pg 34

highest form of worship is to offer your life as dead before a living Lord. To submit our will to His, without questions, we must practice the law of immediate obedience. The words of the apostle Paul are worth repeating. He gives us a view of the life of a person who is fully submitted. The life of a dead man (dead flesh), is the one which has this one response to every thought and action, "Not I, but Christ lives in me." My life operates under the lordship of Jesus. I am intoxicated by His fragrance. I am lifeless without His spirit in me. I have no movement without His breath, no direction unless He commands it. Can you make these declarations? If not yet, get ready. The time is coming.

Far too many of us come to Christ with the baggage of our past and end up missing the assignment the Lord has for us because of the weight we will not let go of, and allow Him to carry. Our own will, desires, feelings and way of thinking never dies and gives way to His, therefore, we miss the fullness of the Christian life. Abundant life mentioned in John 10:10 is not the experience that most Christians have because they refuse to die. When we speak of dying, again we are speaking of putting behind us any old ways or processes of doing things. The whole reality of Christianity is to be born again. It is to rid my life of the old and experience the life God has designed for me to live. You will live your life with the crutches called excuses, until you experience new birth. You will always settle for mediocrity, the assignments, and the things people call you until you truly hear the voice of the one who called you into being. Human beings, devoid of recognition of whose they are, operate in the natural and have no concept of calling things that are not, as though they were. The natural man has no concept of how God operates, calling everything out of the supernatural realm into the natural. So what looks like darkness, confusion, chaos or disorder can be changed at a word from a faith being that sees beyond what a thing is presently. I cannot therefore settle for a person calling my child stupid. I cannot accept anyone calling a young man gay because he was born that way.

I see the darkness, the chaos or confusion, and I speak life into existence. The responsibility of the individual, who has been *labeled* by the natural man, is to accept the word of the supernatural God, experience rebirth, and live the life he or she was ordained to live. Neither the one calling light into the dark world of another, or the one receiving the light and living the "God-said", can do this on their own. You and I need His power to change. In the next chapter we will go through that process, so stay with me. The wait is worth it.

Eventually, as we see the evolution and transformation of our lives into our created worth, we will become a "praise in the earth". Our lives will be Gods' thanks gift. Everywhere we go we will point others to Him, saying, "Hey, I was where you are, but God..."

The goal is to walk in Genesis 1:26-27, *"^{26}Then God said, "Let us make human beings in our image, in our likeness, so that they may rule over the fish in the sea and the birds in the sky, over the livestock and all the wild animals, and over all the creatures that move along the ground." ^{27}So God created human beings in his own image, in the image of God he created them; male and female he created them."*

Can you see yourself walking in the perfect will of God? Do you see yourself being fruitful? Totally submitted? Knowing what you are gifted to do, and then doing it? Walking in love? Living by faith? Teaching others to honor God with everything they have and all they are? Well, I see it for you, until you see it for yourself. As a matter of fact, let's believe God for it, and I will agree with you, that you have *in* you, the capacity to live that kind of life. Say it now, "I have the capacity to live that kind of life and I will do it in Jesus name".

The road to that kind of life will take purposing in your heart to change some things. For some it will take a lot, and for others it may take everything. I can tell you from firsthand experience that the prize is worth far greater than the cost. I cannot tell you how many times I have counted the cost of sin and riotous living that hid behind the cloak of fun. If I had back all of the lost money, time, effort, rest, etc., what could I have accomplished? Thank God for grace. Today I write because I am free. You my dear friend are the beneficiary of my freedom. Who may I ask is the beneficiary of yours?

Art Sepulveda offered this wisdom, "All of God's promises are available to anyone who believes and is willing to pay the price to obtain them. That price is a willingness to fight! Fighting may not sound very Christian, but when it comes to dealing with the enemy of your soul – the devil –, God's word does not endorse meekness or gentleness. It requires a fighting posture, tough, ruthless, bulldog tenacity – because the devil hates you. You are a threat to his plans and purposes, and he will do whatever is necessary to take you out. Your willingness to fight is a matter of survival."[4] We do not like war. But war is necessary. War is the only way that some enemies will surrender in defeat. Death is the only way to victory. Fasting is the key to unleash your full potential, the key to warfare which will produce in you the ability to live the God kind of life. It means to go without food. It means to turn over your plate, refusing to eat. To willingly give up meals to sup with God, so you can overcome the habits formed in this world, and be prepared to live in the world to come (where you will spend eternity). Since you will undoubtedly be there longer than you are here, I would have to say that it *is* worth the fight.

Old Testament Citings

In the Old Testament, there are many examples of fasting that shed light on why we should include it as a practice in our lives. What we will notice is that even unbelievers

---

[4] Art Sepulveda. *How to Live Life on Purpose* Harrison House, Tulsa, OK, 2004 page 193

practiced it as a ritual, expecting results, preparing themselves for an event, or simply as an act of mourning.

Even the apocrypha (inter-testamental writings not accepted as sacred) cites fasting as a way of life to address or overcome sin and cope with seasons of famine. Every religion has its purifying seasons they call times of fasting, yet they draw themselves closer to unknown spirits and idols, not the true and living God revealed in Jesus Christ. In the Old Testament, although they did not have our revelation of Jesus, they knew of their separation from the image they were created in and knew their help in every season was dependant upon an almighty God.

Fourteen considerations are offered to you here. Choose any one as a reason to begin a fast, but make a choice to begin.

I. Public Calamity

II Samuel 1:12 – *"^{12}They mourned and wept and fasted till evening for Saul and his son Jonathan, and for the army of the LORD and the house of Israel, because they had fallen by the sword."*

II Samuel 1:12 offers us the response to the death of a person in authority. When a king dies (a president, head of state or public leader) fasting should arise. When calamity comes to our troops in foreign war then fasting should occur. Who fasts because of the loss of leaders and soldiers today? Note that Saul was not a beloved king at the time. It does not matter whether his/her popularity rating is high or not. His position dictated the response, not his demeanor. If nothing else, fast so that a better choice of leadership is made the next go around.

II. Death of a Loved One

II Samuel 3:35 – *"^{35}Then they all came and urged David to eat something while it was still day; but David took an oath, saying, "May God deal with me, be it ever* *so severely, if I taste bread or anything else before the sun sets!"*

II Samuel 3:35 offers us a view into the life of David. Obviously David practiced fasting. He has to endure the grief of losing several loved ones. His newborn son, his daughter Tamar and his son Absalom, although estranged, has died in battle. No parent should ever have to endure the death of their children. It is not the natural order of things, yet the fall caused many undesirable events to occur in our lives. Death and all of its pain is one of such things. The word of God teaches us not to mourn as others do, having no hope.

I Thessalonians 4:13 – *"[13]Brothers, we do not want you to be ignorant about those who fall asleep, or to grieve like the rest of men, who have no hope."*

Jeremiah 31:13 says, *"[13]...I will turn their mourning into gladness; I will give them comfort and joy instead of sorrow."*

Therefore, we cannot die with the loved one. We cannot become hermits or drown our sorrows in alcoholic beverages. We cannot go on eating binges or shopping binges as a coping method for a bout with depression. David fasted. He separated himself from worldly pleasure and got alone with God to put his pain into perspective. Fasting during the time I was mourning my mother's death, would have been a great medicine for me. It was undoubtedly a season I will never forget. I was lost in excruciating pain. It is seasons like that where you must seek God's help. There is no substitute. The sooner you run to Him the better. It took me a year (and I was in fulltime ministry). The full recovery process may have lasted about fifteen years. A God lead fast would have changed that. It helps you see the vision he has for your life better. It also helps you understand every person's purpose in your life, and how to use what they leave behind for your journey. Their death then becomes a seed for a later harvest in your life.

III. To Meet With God and Receive Revelation

Exodus 24:18 – *"¹⁸Then Moses entered the cloud as he went on up the mountain. And he stayed on the mountain forty days and forty nights."*

Exodus 34:28 – *"²⁸Moses was there with the LORD forty days and forty nights without eating bread or drinking water. And he wrote on the tablets the words of the covenant—the Ten Commandments."*

Deuteronomy 9:9 – *"⁹When I went up on the mountain to receive the tablets of stone, the tablets of the covenant that the LORD had made with you, I stayed on the mountain forty days and forty nights; I ate no bread and drank no water."*

While we will spend more time on this in a later chapter, suffice it to say that *spending* time with God, will often make you *lose* track of time. I have been in my prayer closet for hours and not thought of natural food. The nourishment from heaven was so rich it filled me in ways indescribable. You will look like what you spend time with the most.

IV. To Be In Position to Be Heard By God

Deuteronomy 9:19 – *"¹⁹I feared the anger and wrath of the LORD, for he was angry enough with you to destroy you. But again the LORD listened to me."*

Isaiah 58:9 – *"⁹Then you will call and the LORD will answer; you will cry for help, and he will say: Here am I." If you do away with the yoke of oppression, with the pointing finger and malicious talk..."*

Moses tells the children of Israel his purpose for being on the mountain so long in the Deuteronomy passage. He is careful to tell them that sin has no place in the presence of God. He spends a lengthy time as a sacrifice, lying empty before God on behalf of the people he was called to lead. Is your family worth you lying before the Lord as a sacrifice? Is your company? Is your community worth it? What about your friends? Can you do it for your enemies, so that they can get a revelation of the Christ in you and thereby change their eternal destiny?

The Isaiah passage is a confirmation of Deuteronomy 9:9. The Lord Himself says to the people, if you *fast* properly (note the word, *properly*). There *is* a right and wrong kind of fasting. I will listen to you and respond accordingly. There are some things you will never experience, see, or understand, without proper fasting.

V. To Impress Others and Call the Holy Out

II Kings 19:3-16 – *"³They told him, "This is what Hezekiah says: This day is a day of distress and rebuke and disgrace, as when children come to the point of birth and there is no strength to deliver them. ⁴It may be that the LORD your God will hear all the words of the field commander, whom his master, the king of Assyria, has sent to ridicule the living God, and that he will rebuke him for the words the LORD your God has heard. Therefore pray for the remnant that still survives."*

⁵When King Hezekiah's officials came to Isaiah, ⁶Isaiah said to them, "Tell your master, 'This is what the LORD says: Do not be afraid of what you have heard—those words with which the underlings of the king of Assyria have blasphemed me. ⁷Listen! I am going to put such a spirit in him that when he hears a certain report, he will return to his own country, and there I will have him cut down with the sword.'

"⁸When the field commander heard that the king of Assyria had left Lachish, he withdrew and found the king fighting against Libnah.

⁹Now Sennacherib received a report that Tirhakah, the Cushite king of Egypt, was marching out to fight against him. So he again sent messengers to Hezekiah with this word: ¹⁰"Say to Hezekiah king of Judah: Do not let the god you depend on deceive you when he says, 'Jerusalem will not be handed over to the king of Assyria.' ¹¹Surely you have heard what the kings of Assyria have done to all the countries, destroying them completely. And will you be delivered? ¹²Did the gods of the nations that were destroyed by my forefathers deliver them: the gods of Gozan, Haran, Rezeph and the people of Eden who were in Tel Assar? ¹³Where is the king of Hamath, the king of Arpad, the king of the city of Sepharvaim, or of Hena or Ivvah?"

¹⁴Hezekiah received the letter from the messengers and read it. Then he went up to the temple of the LORD and spread it out before the LORD. ¹⁵And Hezekiah prayed to the LORD: "O

LORD, God of Israel, enthroned between the cherubim, you alone are God over all the kingdoms of the earth. You have made heaven and earth. ¹⁶Give ear, O LORD, and hear; open your eyes, O LORD, and see; listen to the words Sennacherib has sent to insult the living God."

This is not the purpose of a fast. However, even Ahab and Jezebel, the enemies of God fasted and/or at least called one, to identify and expose the righteous. Their sole purpose for calling the fast was singling out the holy so they could extinguish them. On the one hand, fasting is not a tool to impress anyone, but on the other, it will expose your righteousness or unrighteousness. If you want a peek at your flaws or shortcomings, then fasting is a way of exposure. If you truly desire to please the Lord, I highly recommend it to you. *Self-exposure* of sins is far less painful to endure than public exposure. As a matter of fact, the word of God teaches us to judge ourselves, then we do not have to sit awaiting the judgment of others (Matthew 7:2 – *"For in the same way you **judge** others, you will be **judged**, and with the measure you use, it will be measured to you."*) Offer your life as a sacrifice. Do not wait to be crucified because you would not crucify your own flesh.

VI.   For Humility and Safe Journey –

Ezra 8:21-23 – "²¹There, by the Ahava Canal, I proclaimed a fast, so that we might humble ourselves before our God and ask him for a safe journey for us and our children, with all our possessions. ²²I was ashamed to ask the king for soldiers and horsemen to protect us from enemies on the road, because we had told the king, "The gracious hand of our God is on everyone who looks to him, but his great anger is against all who forsake him." ²³So we fasted and petitioned our God about this, and he answered our prayer."

There are times that you are preparing to do things or go places that have the odds stacked against your arriving there. The road to your destination, be it a physical or spiritual one, is lined with enemy distractions. When I was on the road to giving up alcohol, I had friends who said to me, "Hey it's just us here, have one drink with me. No one will know." When you are in the midst of a battle in heavy enemy territory, you need power that only God can give you. Even if you are strong enough, is your children's destiny worth a fast, so that you can see how to give them the direction they need for their journey?

VII. **To Break Generational Curses** –
Nehemiah 9:1-2 – *"¹On the twenty-fourth day of the same month, the Israelites gathered together, fasting and wearing sackcloth and having dust on their heads. ²Those of Israelite descent had separated themselves from all foreigners. They stood in their places and confessed their sins and the wickedness of their fathers."*

The Israelites confessed their own sins, while fasting and separating themselves from anyone that did not line up with their value system. They even confessed the sins of their fathers. We will dig deeper into this in a later chapter, but, know this, you cannot fix what you do not know is broken. Neither can you fix what is broken if you will not admit that it is broken when you see it. Ignoring it will not correct it. It will only infect it. Start at the root or it will return. Do not run from the sins of your fathers. You cannot hide from them. You must face and defeat them or they will find and haunt you. I will see you in chapters five and six concerning this matter.

VIII. For Favor With People In Authority

Esther 4:16 – "*¹⁶"Go, gather together all the Jews who are in Susa, and fast for me. Do not eat or drink for three days, night or day. I and my maids will fast as you do. When this is done, I will go to the king, even though it is against the law. And if I perish, I perish."*

Notice that Esther called a fast, so that she and her people would find favor with the king, even in an off season, where if not summons, a person could be sentenced to death for approaching him. Fasting strengthens you to take risks you would not usually take. It builds your faith to the point that death is an alternative, because you know the aftermath of it is better than this life. It cancels your fear of dying, because you must kill someone who is already dead. You should always remember that fasting kills the flesh (more to come in the next chapter).

IX. To Convert Sinners or Cancel Their Sting

Psalm 35:10-13 – "*¹⁰My whole being will exclaim, "Who is like you, O LORD You rescue the poor from those too strong for them, the poor and needy from those who rob them." ¹¹Ruthless witnesses come forward; they question me on things I know nothing about. ¹²They repay me evil for good and leave my soul forlorn. ¹³Yet when they were ill, I put on sackcloth and humbled myself with fasting."*

Psalm 69:10-13 – "*¹⁰When I weep and fast, I must endure scorn; ¹¹when I put on sackcloth, people make sport of me. ¹²Those who sit at the gate mock me, and I am the song of the *drunkards. ¹³But I pray to you, O LORD, in the time of your favor; in your great love, O God, answer me with your sure salvation."*

These Psalms are called, "Imprecatory" Psalms, and are generally aimed at asking God's wrath on the wicked. However, whenever we are fasting (as well as praying), we are helping to break the bonds of wickedness in ourselves and others according to Isaiah 58. I mention prayer as a partner with the time of fasting, because it is certain that you can pray without fasting, but you can never fast without praying. When we partner these two powerhouses together, the gates of hell begin to tumble. If that be the case, then we should fast regularly for our communities, city and nations to receive the Lord. How badly do you want to see your family members converted? Would not life be easier if all your enemies knew Jesus as Savior and Lord? Even if you begin the fast with a personal reason (found in the second portion of the title), which is to cancel the sting of the enemy, let it be so. *Launch* the fast for *you*, and let the Lord change your misery into a ministry to lead your enemies across the line of faith.

X. For Freedom To Be A Freedom Fighter

Isaiah 58:6-12 – *"⁶"Is not this the kind of fasting I have chosen: to loose the chains of injustice and untie the cords of the yoke, to set the oppressed free and break every yoke?*

⁷Is it not to share your food with the hungry and to provide the poor wanderer with shelter— when you see the naked, to clothe him, and not to turn away from your own flesh and blood?

⁸Then your light will break forth like the dawn, and your healing will quickly appear; then your righteousness will go before you, and the glory of the LORD will be your rear guard.

⁹Then you will call, and the LORD will answer; you will cry for help, and he will say: Here am I. "If you do away with the yoke of oppression, with the pointing finger and malicious talk,

¹⁰and if you spend yourselves in behalf of the hungry and satisfy the needs of the oppressed, then your light will rise in the darkness, and your night will become like the noonday.

¹¹The LORD will guide you always; he will satisfy your needs in a sun-scorched land and will strengthen your frame. You will be like a well-watered garden, like a spring whose waters never fail.

¹²Your people will rebuild the ancient ruins and will raise up the age-old foundations; you will be called Repairer of Broken Walls, Restorer of Streets with Dwellings."

Twelve things happen here as a result of fasting:

1. I Experience Broken Bondage – Personal Freedom

2. I Become a Bondage Breaker – Corporate Anointing

3. The Bread of Life Becomes Me – I eat so much of Him that I become Him to others. They begin to eat of me and live. My words are His Word, and they produce abundant life.

4. I *Cover* the Naked – I do not practice gossip or slander. I cover people with prayer, love and encouragement, until they are able to recover from their naked shame, and get into the place where God is or has called them. Noah's story is an example. He became drunk off of the stuff God gave him, and his mature sons had to cover him until he could return to the place where he had been called by God to be.

5. Revelation (verse 8) – Your eyes will open to things you could not see or understand before. You will read with a new level of comprehension and be encouraged.

6. Restoration (verse 8) – Your physical health will change for the better (further discussed in chapter 8).

7. Righteousness (verse 8) – All of the benefits of righteousness will be yours. You will become who you say you are. You will be mature in the faith, not just called the righteousness of God because you were made that through Jesus' death, but actually living it.

8. Reward (verse 8) – The glory lives in you. You are now a carrier of it. When people see you, they see the Father and follow you so they can come to their destiny. You become the cloud and fire of God that leads people to the promise of God.

9. Response (verse 9) – Your prayer response time is now quicker. The relationship you now have demands immediate response. You are family in

[Margin note: Pray that in all my development, Spiritual maturity and however true maturity in God will bare me is humility, high-minded and pride don't become not pride.]

word and deed. Your righteousness favors you and puts you in position to call and get answered at will.

10. Recognition (verse 10) – Others see you differently. You now lead by your lifestyle. You change the atmosphere in every room you enter.

11. Refreshment (verse 11) – You live with a constant satisfaction. An assurance of His hand keeps you confident in every situation. You live a Psalm 1 life (read it now).

12. Restorer (verse 12) – You have taken on the mantle of Restorer. Having been restored you pay forward what you received from God. Creative power flows through you. The God-kind of DNA is activated and used properly to return people to the image of their true Father.

XI. To Have A Sentence To Be Shortened

Daniel 9:1-19 – "¹In the first year of Darius son of Ahasuerus (a Mede by descent), who was made ruler over the Babylonian kingdom- ²in the first year of his reign, I, Daniel, understood from the Scriptures, according to the word of the LORD given to Jeremiah the prophet, that the desolation of Jerusalem would last seventy years. ³So I turned to the Lord God and pleaded with him in prayer and petition, in fasting, and in sackcloth and ashes.

⁴I prayed to the LORD my God and confessed: "O Lord, the great and awesome God, who keeps his covenant of love with all who love him and obey his commands, ⁵we have sinned and

done wrong. We have been wicked and have rebelled; we have turned away from your commands and laws. ⁶We have not listened to your servants the prophets, who spoke in your name to our kings, our princes and our fathers, and to all the people of the land.

⁷"Lord, you are righteous, but this day we are covered with shame—the men of Judah and people of Jerusalem and all Israel, both near and far, in all the countries where you have scattered us because of our unfaithfulness to you. ⁸O LORD, we and our kings, our princes and our fathers are covered with shame because we have sinned against you. ⁹The Lord our God is merciful and forgiving, even though we have rebelled against him; ¹⁰we have not obeyed the LORD our God or kept the laws he gave us through his servants the prophets. ¹¹All Israel has transgressed your law and turned away, refusing to obey you.

"Therefore the curses and sworn judgments written in the Law of Moses, the servant of God, have been poured out on us, because we have sinned against you. ¹²You have fulfilled the words spoken against us and against our rulers by bringing upon us great disaster. Under the whole heaven nothing has ever been done like what has been done to Jerusalem. ¹³Just as it is written in the Law of Moses, all this disaster has come upon us, yet we have not sought the favor of the LORD our God by turning from our sins and giving attention to your truth. ¹⁴The LORD did not hesitate to bring the disaster upon us,

for the LORD our God is righteous in everything he does; yet we have not obeyed him

[15]"Now, O Lord our God, who brought your people out of Egypt with a mighty hand and who made for yourself a name that endures to this day, we have sinned, we have done wrong. [16]O Lord, in keeping with all your righteous acts, turn away your anger and your wrath from Jerusalem, your city, your holy hill. Our sins and the iniquities of our fathers have made Jerusalem and your people an object of scorn to all those around us

[17]"Now, our God, hear the prayers and petitions of your servant. For your sake, O Lord, look with favor on your desolate sanctuary. [18]Give ear, O God, and hear; open your eyes and see the desolation of the city that bears your Name. We do not make requests of you because we are righteous, but because of your great mercy. [19]O Lord, listen! O Lord, forgive! O Lord, hear and act! For your sake, O my God, do not delay, because your city and your people bear your Name."

Daniel begins a time of prayer and fasting to have the sentence of desolation of Jerusalem lessened from 70 years. The bible says of curses, that they go to the third generation. They can be broken *during*, and *after* a time of fasting. You may be experiencing a set time of incarceration in the natural, spiritual, emotional or financial realm and need an early release. Get started on a fast. Your breakthrough may come merely in the form of stress release or peace that passes understanding, but you *will* get a release.

XII. To Gain Understanding/Revelation/Vision

Daniel 10:1-7 – "*[1] In the third year of Cyrus king of Persia, a revelation was given to Daniel (who was called Belteshazzar). Its message was true and it concerned a great war. The understanding of the message came to him in a vision*

[2] At that time I, Daniel, mourned for three weeks. [3] I ate no choice food; no meat or wine touched my lips; and I used no lotions at all until the three weeks were over.

[4] On the twenty-fourth day of the first month, as I was standing on the bank of the great river, the Tigris, [5] I looked up and there before me was a man dressed in linen, with a belt of the finest gold around his waist. [6] His body was like chrysolite, his face like lightning, his eyes like flaming torches, his arms and legs like the gleam of burnished bronze, and his voice like the sound of a multitude

[7] I, Daniel, was the only one who saw the vision; the men with me did not see it, but such terror overwhelmed them that they fled and hid themselves."

Joel 2:12-17 – "[12] *"Even now," declares the LORD, "return to me with all your heart, with fasting and weeping and mourning."*

[13] *Rend your heart and not your garments. Return to the LORD your God, for he is gracious and compassionate, slow to anger and*

abounding in love, and he relents from sending calamity.

¹⁴Who knows? He may turn and have pity and leave behind a blessing—grain offerings and drink offerings for the LORD your God.

¹⁵Blow the trumpet in Zion, declare a holy fast, call a sacred assembly.

¹⁶Gather the people, consecrate the assembly; bring together the elders, gather the children, those nursing at the breast. Let the bridegroom leave his room and the bride her chamber.

¹⁷Let the priests, who minister before the LORD, weep between the temple porch and the altar. Let them say, "Spare your people, O LORD. Do not make your inheritance an object of scorn, a byword among the nations. Why should they say among the peoples, 'Where is their God?' "

There are times in your life when you are clueless about: where you are headed; what the enemy has thrown at you; and how to overcome it. In those seasons of war over your very existence, you need a revelation. There are times when you dream and you know there is something in the dream for your life, but you cannot comprehend it. You need understanding, but you cannot concentrate because the things going on around you keep you preoccupied. You need help blocking out your distractions and your circumstances. You need a vision of things to come, so you can see hope in the midst of whatever situation you find yourself. Fasting will open the eyes of your understanding.

XIII. For Corporate Repentance, To Restore That Which Was Lost

Joel 1:12-14 – "*^{12}The vine is dried up and the fig tree is withered; the pomegranate, the palm and the apple tree—all the trees of the field—are dried up. Surely the joy of mankind is withered away.*

^{13}Put on sackcloth, O priests, and mourn; wail, you who minister before the altar. Come, spend the night in sackcloth, you who minister before my God; for the grain offerings and drink offerings are withheld from the house of your God.

^{14}Declare a holy fast; call a sacred assembly. Summon the elders and all who live in the land to the house of the LORD your God, and cry out to the LORD."

When a dry season comes as a result of undisciplined or unrestrained lives, the intercessors, those who are true believers and kingdom caretakers are called to gather at the house of God and make a corporate declaration of a holy fast and prayer meeting. It is the calling together of the mature, to stand in agreement for repentance, until reversal of plagues, curses, corruption and destruction end. This fast, called a Holy fast, indicates that you should be careful to do nothing devoted to yourself. Everything done is devoted to God. It may mean the cutting off of every secular pleasure, to gain God's attention and to gain your attention to Him alone (television, radio, phones, e-mail or work). These fasts may be short. They may also be at times when people are off of work (Friday until Sunday), or on scheduled days away at a retreat. Be prepared for a shift in the spirit realm when fasting takes on this level.

This kind of fasting will be difficult. The degree to which you fast however, will determine the shift in your spiritual life.

XIV. To Save a City

Jonah 3:1-10 – *"¹Then the word of the LORD came to Jonah a second time: ²"Go to the great city of Nineveh and proclaim to it the message I give you."*

³Jonah obeyed the word of the LORD and went to Nineveh. Now Nineveh was a very important city—a visit required three days. ⁴On the first day, Jonah started into the city. He proclaimed: "Forty more days and Nineveh will be overturned." ⁵The Ninevites believed God. They declared a fast, and all of them, from the greatest to the least, put on sackcloth

⁶When the news reached the king of Nineveh, he rose from his throne, took off his royal robes, covered himself with sackcloth and sat down in the dust. ⁷Then he issued a proclamation in Nineveh: "By the decree of the king and his nobles: Do not let any man or beast, herd or flock, taste anything; do not let them eat or drink. ⁸But let man and beast be covered with sackcloth. Let everyone call urgently on God. Let them give up their evil ways and their violence. ⁹Who knows? God may yet relent and with compassion turn from his fierce anger so that we will not perish."

¹⁰When God saw what they did and how they turned from their evil ways; he had compassion and did not bring upon them the destruction he had threatened."

A. To Hear The Voice of God Clearly and Obey.

B. To Hold Off Destruction After It Has Been Pronounced.

The Ninevites called a fast and even put their animals on the fast. If their animals were on it, don't you think we should begin to help our children learn this discipline for their future welfare too? What are you willing to do to get your city saved? What is your hearing like? Are you hearing God clearly? If not, then fasting will help you. Let's gain further understanding as we move to chapter 3. There we will learn why we do this thing called fasting, so we can prepare ourselves for a breakthrough to another spiritual dimension of grace and kingdom work.

3
Types of Fasts: Designing the Fast for Your Need

> *"Nothing can truly prepare you for your first fast because you have never seen distractions like you will see. On the other hand, nothing will satisfy you like the joy you receive from it when you have broken through and completed (really completed) your first one."*
> *Bishop Darryl F. Husband*

Well, if you have arrived this far, you are ready to put your new weapon to work. By now, your flesh is tense because it is getting ready to lose its position as your master. Satan is furious that you are reading through this book and are now in preparation for dominion restoration. However, preparation is not manifestation, so stay excited enough to start and complete the journey, not just to fast, but to having a fasted life. That is the conqueror's lifestyle. The life of an overcomer has your picture as its poster child. You are the kingdom representative, the spokesperson for "world overcomers".

In this chapter we will do four things:

1) Help you prepare for your time of fasting. There are a few areas of your life in which you need to check up on to prepare yourself;

2) Explore some of the different types of fasts recorded in scripture;

3) Give you medical cautions or considerations, and finally

4) Give you instruction on how to get started as well as how to move to successful completion.

Every fast does not end in successful completion. Some just end in completion. I quit is a form of completion. It is just not successful. I am cheering for your success. I wrote this book with you in mind. I only wish someone had saved me from the reckless path I pursued for many years. I honestly believe that the culture in which I grew up (in ministry) didn't know much better than to live like we lived. We were so entrenched in the institution called preaching and the preacher, that we could not see that God was calling us to *be* the Church. He was depending on us to believe, preach, and then live the Word. We took to another level, what we saw and learned from our mentors and fathers in the faith. They were strong powerful men of God. They knew one way, and that was the traditions of their forefathers. I am in no way here, to put them on trial. I am here to escort you, as I had to be escorted, out of the clutches of what may have been handed down to you. After reading this book you no longer have an excuse to fall back into traditional, carnal, half committed, only in church, Christian living.

The Four Areas of Preparation

I.   The first step of your preparation is ***Spiritually***. Prepare yourself spiritually. Before you get started with your fast, let's read some scripture and make some confessions. As you can tell by now, I believe the Word of God is a key to your present and future life. Confessions build your faith and steer you into the righteous direction you were born to pursue. So let's get started. Please read the following aloud and make them personal.

  A. I Corinthians 6:19 – *"¹⁹Do you not know that your body is a temple of the Holy Spirit, who is in you, whom you have received from God? You are not your own"*— My body is the temple of the Holy Spirit.

  B. I Corinthians 9:37 – *"²⁷... I beat my body and make it my slave so that after I have preached to others, I myself will not be disqualified for the prize"* — I beat my body daily. I discipline myself. I will not allow myself to be controlled by things in the world. I will not preach to others, what I do not believe myself. I live so as not to be disqualified on the Day of Judgment.

  C. I Corinthians 6:13 – *"¹³"Food for the stomach and the stomach for food"—but God will destroy them both. The body is not meant for sexual immorality, but for the Lord, and the Lord for the body"* — My body belongs to the Lord and the Lord is for my body.

  D. II Timothy 1:7 – *"⁷For God did not give us a spirit of timidity, but a spirit of power, of love and of self-discipline"* — God has not given me the spirit of fear. I have a sound mind. I walk in the power of God. I am a product of love and therefore I speak the love of Christ wherever I go.

  E. I John 5:4 – *"⁴for everyone born of God overcomes the world. This is the victory that has overcome the world, even our faith"* — I have overcome the world.

F. I eat to live I do not live to eat.

G. My weight is under control.

H. I crave the will of God for my life.

I. No (*you fill in this blank*), has a right to tell me what to do.

J. I am a picture of health and the Lord gets glory out of my body.

K. I have more energy than ever, because I eat right and live right.

L. I shall live and not die.

M. Whatever I put my mind to it is a done deal.

N. I have the mind of Christ and no weapon formed against me shall prosper.

Matthew 9:15 says, *"[15]Jesus answered, "How can the guests of the bridegroom mourn while he is with them? The time will come when the bridegroom will be taken from them; then they will fast"*. Notice Jesus said that the day would come when He was gone. This is when the disciples should fast, longing for Him. In the Song of Solomon 5:8, the scripture says, *"[8]O daughters of Jerusalem, I charge you—if you find my lover, what will you tell him? Tell him I am faint with love."*

The life of the child of God always longs for the presence of their groom (creator). Two things to note concerning the Matthew passage: 1) when you feel empty of Him in any areas of your life, fasting is the answer; 2) if He is not Lord over an area, fast until He is (marriage, family, finances, attitude, eating habits, submitting to authority etc.). Use the following as an additional help:

   a) Ask for and continually thank God for His Help.
   b) Read Isaiah 58 and keep in front of you the rewards of fasting (Mike Bickle's book on that subject is helpful as well).
   c) Keep your confessions in your mouth throughout the fast.
   d) Write down a list of other scriptures and topics you need to read about, things you need that will minister to you.
   e) Get some prayer books (*The Altared Life*, by me!).
   f) Set your prayer times and menu or agenda. Know what you are intending to pray for and about and what time you will begin and end (if you have to).

II. Prepare yourself *Mentally*. This sounds so close to the first preparation but it is different. If you prepare spiritually, undoubtedly, you are preparing your mind, but I want you to take this a step further.

   A. Use mental pictures. See yourself on the other side of the fast. See yourself after completion. You have confessed it now see it. Now write it. Draw it. Somehow get a picture of the you that you are fasting to become. Or, see the city you are fasting for as crime free or drug free.

B. Read the testimony in the last chapter to motivate you. You gain faith by hearing. Read it at least one time aloud.

C. Read Matthew 6:16, 18 – *"^{16}"When you fast, do not look somber as the hypocrites do, for they disfigure their faces to show men they are fasting. I tell you the truth, they have received their reward in full. ^{18}so that it will not be obvious to men that you are fasting, but only to your Father, who is unseen; and your Father, who sees what is done in secret, will reward you."* It says "when you fast", not "if" you do, God will reward you. Trust that and go get your rewards. See them, say them and then move forward until you arrive at where they are.

III. Prepare yourself **Emotionally and Socially**. All of these are so closely related yet I believe this is the most difficult one for busy and interactive people. If you are an extrovert (a person who is outgoing, friendly or people person) you will find this as the area of challenge. There are a few things you may have to consider as your prepare in this area.

A. Who your true friends are?

B. What are you so tied to that it will pain you to distance yourself from?

C. How will you deal with cravings and criticism?

D. How do you handle being alone with God? Fasting can be corporate, but it is often individual in nature. It is about you and Him.

IV. Preparing you *Physically*. Since you know the fast is coming (unless it is a "suddenly" fast, orchestrated by God commanded to start now), then there are some things you can do to prepare yourself. Your body usually goes through some withdrawals when you first begin a fast. It goes through withdrawals for sugar, coffee (caffeine) etc. Sometimes there are headaches, stomach pains, energy losses, but all are usually in the first days of a fast. Your body is crying out to have what you are addicted to, bust as a drug addict's body does. The question is, "Will you give in?" **NO!** Here is my suggestion, slowly wean yourself off of anything you crave daily. Do not have it in as large a proportion as you usually would. Often, right before Lent, people do go out and celebrate what is called, "fat Tuesday". This is the day when you go out and eat all the things you are not suppose to on your fast. I used to participate in this faithfully, in my first years of fasting. However, I found this *ritual* to be harmful rather than harmless. Instead of a celebration, it was feeding my addiction to sweets and causing deeper withdrawals the day the fast began. It was tantamount to an alcoholic saying, "I am going to quit tomorrow, so I will just go out tonight and drink the best tasting, most expensive liquor I can find to prepare me for my sobriety." Do not laugh! It is not funny. Okay, well maybe it is. Or, maybe it is a little crazy.

Reasons, Periods and Types of Fasts

A. Eight (8) Reasons for Fasts Recorded In Scripture (A Brief Reminder). Let's begin with the longest to the shortest.

1. Power over Demons (Mark 9:29 KJV)
2. Prophetic Revelation (Daniel 9, 10, 11)
3. Salvation and Preparation for Ministry (Acts 9:15, Acts 13:1, 2)
4. Reversal of Cities Destruction (Joel 1, 2, Deuteronomy 9:7-21)

       5. Protection (Daniel 6:18-23, Ezra 8:21-21, Esther 4:16)
       6. Direction to Ministry (Acts 14:23)
       7. Preparation for Bridegroom (Matthew 9:14-15)
       8. Overcoming the Flesh (Daniel 1:5-20)

  B.   Six (6) biblical periods of time for fasting

       1. Moses, Elijah and Jesus Fasted for 40 Days (Extended) – (Exodus 24:18, 34:28; I Kings 19:8; Matthew 4:2,3)
       2. Daniel Fasted for 21 Days (Daniel 10:2-3)
       3. David Fasted for 7 Days – (II Samuel 12:15, 18, 21-23)
       4. Paul Fasted for 3 Days – (Acts 9:9)
       5. Levitical Fast – 1 Day (Leviticus 16:29; 23:27)
       6. Jesus, John and Anna Fasted Life (Matthew 3:4; Luke 2:36-37; Mark 9:29)

C. Six (6) Types of Fasting

    1. Complete Fast: Nothing! This should never last but a few days. The body will die without water.
    2. Partial Fast – The Daniel fast is a partial fast. No meats, but fruit and vegetables.
    3. Water Fast – The human body must have water. There are times when you should take a few days to completely cleanse your body and allow God to cleanse your spirit.
    4. Fruit and Vegetable Juice Fast – You will need a juicer. IF you purchase it, it will be worth it. Juiced fruit and vegetable are excellent for healing and health. All of the vitamins and nutrients are in the juice. They get lost when cooked.
    5. Media Fast – You cut off internet, television, radio, phones (unless an emergency).

6. Word Fast – No words, Vow of Silence. You may only do this for a half a day or so unless you go away on a retreat. You will not speak any negative words. You will hear the word of God, read the word of God and say the word of God, only.

D. Things to Do During and After the Fast

1. During the fast:

- Dress warmly – you can expect to feel colder during a fast, especially in your hands and feet
- Use warm, not hot, water for showers and baths
- Avoid ice cold beverages
- Exercise regularly, but moderately – if you experience weakness, discontinue
- Fast in secret – don't walk around boasting that you are fasting; it is between you and the Lord.

2. After the fast:

- Avoid starches for a few days
- Chew your food well
- Stop eating when you feel full
- Don't become physically active too soon
- Eat healthy food

3. Medical Perspective on Fasting

Physicians with a spiritual orientation tend to be more inclined than others to employee fasting, both personally and medically. In Spiritual Nutrition and the Rainbow Diet, Gabriel Cousens, M.D., a California physician and spiritual teacher, includes an excellent chapter on fasting in which he describes his concepts of fasting and his own 40-day fast. According to Dr. Cousens,

...fasting in a larger context, means to abstain from that which is toxic to mind, body, and soul. A way to understand this is that fasting is the elimination of physical, emotional, and mental toxins from our organism, intake. Fasting for spiritual purposes usually involves some degree of removal of oneself from worldly responsibilities. It can mean complete silence and social isolation during the fast, which can be a great revival to those of us who have been putting our energy outward.

Other Aspects of Healthy Fasting

- **Fresh air**—plenty is needed to support cleansing and oxygenation of the cells and tissues.
- **Sunshine**—also needed to revitalize our body; avoid excessive exposure.
- **Water**—bathing is very important to cleanse the skin at least twice daily. Steams and saunas are also good for giving warmth as well as supporting detoxification.
- **Skin brushing**—with a dry, soft brush prior to bathing; this will help clear toxins from the skin. This is a good year-round practice as well.
- **Exercise**—very important to support the cleansing process. It helps to relax the body, clear wastes, and prevent toxicity symptoms. Walking, bicycling, swimming, or other

usual exercises can usually be done during a fast, although more dangerous or contact sports might be avoided.

- **No drugs**—none should be used during fasts except mandatory prescription drugs. Particularly, avoidance of alcohol, nicotine, and caffeine is wise.
- **Vitamin supplements**—these should not be used during fasting;
- **Colon cleansing**—an essential part of healthy fasting. Some form of bowel stimulation is recommended. Whatever colon cleansing method is used, keep in mind that regular cleansing of the intestines and colon is a key component to healthy and stress-free fasting.
- **Work and be creative**—and make plans for your life. Staying busy is helpful in breaking our ties to food. We also need time for ourselves. Most fasters experience greater work energy and more creativity and, naturally, find lots to do.
- **Cleanup**—a motto during fasting. As we clean our body, we want to clean our room, desk, office, closes, and home—just like "spring cleaning". It clearly brings us into harmony with the cleansing process of nutrition. If we want to get ready for the new, we need to make space by cleaning out the old.
- **Joining others** in fasting can guarantee strong bonds and provide an added spiritual lift. It opens up new supportive relationships and new levels of existing ones. It will also provide support if we feel down or want to quit. Most people feel better as their fast progresses—more vital, lighter, less blocked, more flexible, clearer, and more spiritually attuned. For many, it is nice to have someone with whom to share this.
- **Avoid the negative influence** of others who may not understand or support us. There are many fears and misconceptions about fasting, and they may affect us. We need to listen to our own inner guidance and not to others' limitations, but we also need to maintain awareness and insight into any problems should they arise.

- **The economy** of fasting allows us to save time, money, and future health care costs. While we may be worried about not having enough, we may already have too much. Many of us are inspired to share more of ourselves when we are freed from food.
- **Meditation and relaxation** are also an important aspect of fasting to help attune us to deeper levels of ourselves and clear the stresses that we have carried with us.
- **Spiritual practice and prayer** will affirm our positive attitude toward life and ourselves in general. This supports our meditation and relaxation and provides us with the inner fuel to carry on our life with purpose and passion.

Tips for Successful Completion

A.   Create a R.O.S.E.

1. Rationale – know why you are fasting. Be settled on why you are doing this, even if it's out of obedience to your spiritual authority. It may be because you have some areas that need breaking. It may be because your city is in trouble. See the list noted in this and previous chapters.

2. Objective – What is your goal or and your goals? What do you want to see happen as a result of your fast? Post them as expectations.

3. Strategies – How are you going to accomplish the goals? What will you do to attack the issues? Pray? Write? Read up on, confess or get counseling? Make a

budget? Cut the television off or turn off part of cable channels, etc.?

    4. Evaluation – Before you quit fasting or come off, ask yourself have you accomplished your goals. If not, try again with new strategies. If so, celebrate with testimony and teaching others to do the same. Write your story for someone else to read.

B.   Remember "Daniel" and be patient if you don't see immediate results. In Chapter 10 of Daniel, we see that it took 21 days into the fast before he got a revelation.

C.   If you break the fast, do not quit. Begin again immediately. Satan is fighting for your failure. You must fight for your breakthrough. It is worth it.

D.   Prepare your scriptures that deal with the areas of your need and read, read and read. Get faith for the new you, the new city or whatever you want to see.

E.   Have that talk with your friends about your time alone with God. Tell them you will be better as a friend when your resurface. Be careful, though, you might discover that some were not really friends after all.

F.   Tape your television shows if you need to. Who knows, you may delete them for lack of interest after the fast.

G.   Shop for the foods you need during the fast and remove any other temptations from your sight if you must.

H.   Store away books, magazines and anything else that you would not want Jesus to see if He came to your house. Some of those store aways will one day become throw aways.

I.   Write a servants list. What things or people you want to serve or bless during this time? Is there anyone you need to love on, forgive, pray for, visit or ask forgiveness?

J.   Practice some Random Acts of Kindness.

K.   Download, purchase or prepare the music you need to listen to during the fast. Atmosphere for arrival at your destination is significant.

4
Starving the Flesh

> *"If thou wouldst preserve a sound body, use fasting and walking; if a healthful soul, fasting and praying. Walking exercises the body; praying exercises the soul. Fasting cleanses both."*
> Francis Quarles (1592-1644, English poet)

In my book on the *"Altared Life"*, I share my testimony about a 21-day period in my journey that broke me through to personal revival. I am convinced that I would never have written this book or that one had I not had that experience. There are some things in your life you will never get a release to do until you settle some other things. You cannot hear or see or focus in some areas because your desires for the world cloud your view to seeing the path to reach potential fulfillment. Visions and dreams will surface and flashes of excitement result. You may even accomplish some things that others have not, and be content. Yet, your full potential cannot truly be seen and be operated in until you have submitted solely to God. It is the, "not as I will, but thy will be done", defining moment in your life that propels you to death, so that others might live. Notice that I used "propels you to death", because this death is an elevation like the cross was for Jesus. He rose up to die. His willingness to die gave birth to something new. It gave birth to the church, to me, to a revelation of life, service and love unparalleled.

> In the *"Altared Life"*, I write, *"It was not prayer alone that got me this "altared" life, this life under total submission to the will of God; this life fully desirous of communing with God all day long about everything. Mark 9:17-29, tells the story of a father who brought his son to the Disciples of Christ and they could not heal him. After much discussion and inquiring by the disciples, Jesus shared why they could not heal this boy. He said, "Some things only come by fasting and praying."(KJV). The flesh must be overtaken by the spirit, by starving it. Starve the flesh, feed the spirit with Word and pray for revelation. This gives behavior-conquering power to you. My life has never been the same. Fasting and praying have partnered to give me identification and integrity, language and lifestyle, tongues and temperament. For 21 days I turned off the world of television, newspaper and radio. I shut the secular world completely off so I could hear from God. I cut out foods and drinks containing any body altering substance. I wanted to only be moved by the presence of God. Finally, I experienced true flesh submission."*[5]

The key to this kind of life is starving the flesh. Let's investigate what that means. What is our oldest habit? You

---

[5] Darryl F. Husband, *The Altared Life*, Lulu.Com, 2008, pg 10-11

must agree that it is eating. For far too many people, eating is an addiction. The first few (typically 9) months of our lives (in the mother's womb), we eat what she eats whether it is good or bad. It is said, and rightfully so, that our early years are our formative years. Some have suggested that whatever we are to become, is often the product of our early childhood eating habits, and learned behavioral functions. Our attachment to sweets is done at an early age. Drug addict mothers pass on addictions to their unborn children through the umbilical cord. The first nourishment of children comes through their parents. So then, if our children are not healthy or become obese (fat or overweight), or have high sugar (diabetes) is it not the fault of undisciplined adults? I have become a student of a healthy life style. As I have studied health books from medical doctors who are Christians, I have discovered the importance of monitoring what we do and do not eat, and what time of day it is, as well as what time or season of the year.

    Eating involves our wants, desires and our will. It is, as we indicated continuously, developed as a habit from conception. Years of development happen in this area before we have a personal say in the matter. Our wills are often forced upon us by unknowing or addicted parents, who pass on unhealthy habits from their parents or grandparents.

    In order to deal with this unhealthy habit, we must find a way to break it. We must break the cycle of what we do, until we are free from craving it. There are several ways of breaking habits. One way is the weaning oneself off of the thing. That is, slowly cutting back on it until you can do without it. The second way is to substitute something for the thing you are giving up. Find something that is *as* satisfying to you, but not destructive, and replace the other. The third way is to simply go "cold turkey", and quit. This last method often takes greater will and divine help. Developing new ways of eating or doing anything after doing those things one way for a long time, takes work.

To understand the dynamics of this, it is important to know how we are made up. You see, this is not really about food, but life and how it will be governed. We began with food because it is the first and foremost area of which you use your *will*. If you can conquer foods, you can order your future. It is that simple. Food is connected to your future. In the rest of this chapter we will see how.

You and I are tri-part beings. We are Spirit, Soul and Body. We are made in the image of God and given His Spirit which is suppose to lead and govern our activities in time, so that we can be led without crippling failures, into eternity. We have a soul which consists of the mind, will and emotions. In the perfect order of things, the Spirit guides the way we think, what we desire, and the way we feel. In a fallen or disobedient/rebellious, God dishonoring (ignoring) state, the soul goes about to establish its own righteousness (right way of living). As you can see, we are back to Genesis (in the bible). We have the capacity for "the tree of life" and "the tree of knowledge of good and evil", just like our creator God. What we choose to eat determines our future, Him or self-pleasure, which is a form of idol worship. The majority of human kind has chosen the latter. We have become a society of "self-worshippers". Me first, God second is the order of the day. Therefore, death is the end result. It is so because a law is broken. "Thou shall have no other god before Me (God)." That includes you. You can become your own god. You can foolishly begin to worship yourself and the things you have.

The body is the house of the spirit and soul of a human. It is strengthened or weakened by what we eat. It is affected by both the spirit and the soul. It will eventually come to an end, but how it ends, (what shape it is in) is determined by whom and how it is governed.

Matthew's gospel records Jesus asking the Father whether that which He came to do could be changed (Matthew 26:39-43). After prayer, He made a decision to deny his will (earthly flesh), and declare that the will of the Father be done.

He said, "*Watch and pray so that you will not fall into temptation. The spirit is willing, but the body (soulish man that influences the body) is weak.*"

When the flesh or soul (mind, will, and emotions) is strong, it chooses to put in its body junk food or non-nutritional substances that steal its ability to live long (healthy, wealthy and wise). It chooses satisfaction in time, without consideration of eternity. It never weighs the two, then making a decision which one would be most beneficial for it to prepare. You are here now, pursuing knowledge and understanding on how to weaken the soul and strengthen the spirit. That sounds strange. A strong soul however, means that your mind, will and emotions control your life. You act completely on worldly knowledge, what you want (whether it is good for you or not). You spend a lot of time trying to live off of what commercials have advertised and made attractive to you. Your feelings go up and down based upon your mood. They are affected by fluctuating circumstances—(weather, how you are treated by others, time of day, amount of rest, whether you have been affirmed by your significant other or not).

This is not to suggest that you do not read or advance your education. It is simply saying that *you* are god, or *God* is God. His spirit rules your life or your soul rules. You have either chosen the tree of life or the tree of knowledge of good and evil. You must choose. Make sure it is based upon intense investigation of the advantages and/or consequences of your choice.

I want to suggest and firmly advise the life tree. It will entail the starving of your flesh. To grow up the spirit man as the dominant force in your existence you <u>must</u> starve, refuse to feed, the "soulish" man, the flesh, until he yields as a slave, to the spirit man's authority. To see that happen you will have to look at the concept of working out (yes, exercising) for the first time. There are four things I see that you need.

I. Visualization of the Goal

If you cannot see it, you probably will not become it (at least not on purpose). What you cannot see, you will at best have a lackadaisical pursuit towards. What is it you believe God has uniquely birthed you to do? When is the last time you dreamed of being it? I mean day-dreaming where you can dress the scene, the life, just the way it is suppose to be?

Leighton Ford says that, "vision is like a magnifying glass which creates focus, a bridge which takes us from the present to the future, a target that beckons". [6] When you see yourself the way God sees you and compare that image to your present one, it should cause you to demand a change of yourself (since you are His and not your own).

Using the same analogy we mentioned about working out (exercising), visualization is critical when you are out of shape. Pull out some old pictures of the healthiest you that you can find. If you have never been a very healthy person, find someone to model. Draw a picture. The same is so for your spiritual life. However, there is only one model. Jesus is our prototype. It is time to get in shape and stay in shape, so let's continue.

II. Commitment to Overcoming Temptations

In my book on the *Altared Life*, I suggest the fact that discipline is important. One way to fight off temptation and distractions is to get on a schedule. Plan what you are going to do and how (read the section on "Make an Appointment"). The old adage is true, if you fail to plan, you plan to fail. If you are trying to quit eating sweets, but you keep writing it on your grocery list, picking it up and hiding it in the back of the refrigerator so you can't see it often, you have failed already.

---

[6] Leighton Ford, *Transforming Leadership*, InterVarsity Press, Downers Grove, Il, 1991, pg 100.

Unless you *schedule* a workout, you will not generally surprise yourself with one. Write in your time with your family. Do not go to the bar to socialize with your friends. Write out every temptation, every possible thing that could hinder you from accomplishing your goals and then…

III. Want the End Results More Than Your Present Position

I recall so vividly my fight to get clean from alcohol and cigarettes. I was not labeled as an alcoholic or a smoker by most people. But amongst a hidden crowd of friends I chained smoked while I consumed alcohol more than the law allowed. What a merciful God we serve! As I came to a greater revelation of Christ (the Anointed One and His Anointing) in me, I grew ashamed, then agitated, with having allowed myself to travel that far away from God. I let my agitation take me to the place of anointing. When you are strengthened, help someone else. Do not settle for being a spiritual dwarf when a giant life is available.

In the book, *"Wake Up Your Dreams"*, Walt Kallestad writes, *"Capturing the dream is like digging for gold. On the surface, the ground may look like nothing more than a pile of rocks or a weed-infested plot. Deep down, however, lies a treasure waiting to be discovered. To uncover it requires much digging and hard work. That's what capturing the dream is all about— digging to discover the treasure of our dreams. We may have to dig very deep, and we may have to work long and hard before our dream dig pays off.*

No great dream is superficial or a mere fantasy. Great dreams require digging beyond surface limitations or past failures or easy-way-out distractions. Dreamers must be actively, passionately digging to bring to light the treasure of their dreams." [7]

Fight my dear friend. Dig deep, until you discover gold. Starve the flesh until it submits to the spirit. Desire the best in you to rise up and live.

IV.   Be Prepared to Do It Alone

You *may* have a friend who is pursuing the same path, but you may not. This is not about anyone else. This is about *your* health alone. You will appear before the Lord at judgment *without* your parents or guardians, spouse or co-workers.

My daughter in ministry, Sandra Johnson, gave me a great book called, *Swimming Lessons* by Grant Edwards. In chapter 9 of his book, he talks about the essential discipline of Evangelism, but I saw it relating to how every Christian should govern their life. He shares that competitive swimmers are different from other athletes. That often they must do without the perks other athletes get and take for granted. They rarely experience crowds, cheers, or pep rallies. They also have to eat differently. He writes, *"Swimmers are the ones who can't party past midnight because they have to be in the water at 6:00 the next morning, getting in their laps. While their friends are chowing down on nachos, simmers have to pass on. Why? Because in the pool every extra ounce is like a boat anchor."*

Swimmers discipline their bodies and adjust their schedules. They find themselves constantly explaining why they can't do something—or why they must do something—and the explanation is always the same: "I'm a swimmer" [8]

---

[7] Walter P. Kallestad, *Wake Up Your Dreams*, Zondervan Publishing House, Grand Rapids, MI, 1996, pg 12.

[8] Grant Edwards, *Swimming Lessons, How to Keep Christians Afloat in a Sinking World*, Specificity Publishing, Springfield OH, pg 128

I believe this applies to us as believers. We are often not the most recognizable citizens in society, but indeed very important. We are the silent captain that is called to steer the ship to shore, through the turbulent seas of life. We are different. We cannot spend our lives in the dining halls, stuffing ourselves with worldly weight, yet expecting to stay awake or alert. We are called to early rising and training and careful intake of things because we do not want to gain any excess weight that will burden us or cause us slothfulness, as we move to wherever God calls us to move. We also must be prepared to be as Paul was in the 9th chapter of the book of Acts. He had to be alone with the Lord to get a revelation of who he was, and what he was called to do. This is a difficult thing to do. We often like crowds. We like the full gym. We enjoy working out with a team or a friend. But the best of athletes know that there are days you cannot be motivated by others. You must at times, get up and go through training alone, against your own will, solely for purpose of accomplishing the goals you set.

Soul Food

In order to properly attack the beast, you have to know what it feeds off of. Again, the soul (flesh) consists of our way of thinking, desires/wants and our feelings. I have to know what it is that feeds these areas of my life so that I can monitor what comes in. What nourishes the thinking, wants or feelings in me? Here are a few of the nourishing things: television, radio, newspapers, magazines, books, Internet, music CDs and friends. Nehemiah 9:1-2 says, *"[1]On the twenty-fourth day of the same month, the Israelites gathered together, fasting and wearing sackcloth and having dust on their heads. [2]Those of Israelite descent had separated themselves from all foreigners. They stood in their places and confessed their sins and the wickedness of their fathers."* Notice they had separated themselves from all foreigners while they were fasting. Anything that cannot be considered as acceptable to God should be cut off. Here is a good rule of thumb. Whenever you are preparing to do something, ask yourself, could you invite Jesus, and would He be comfortable?

In reality, everything we have in life affects the soul. Whatever we do with whatever we are given has eternal consequences. Let's investigate these food categories.

Television

The number one "soul" feeder in America has to be the television. Daily we are told what to do and how to do it by watching something on television. Note, that it tells us what vision we should have. It helps us sculpt our lives. It is very true, "life does imitate art". Have you ever noticed the change in television today and twenty or thirty years ago? How has sexuality been affected? What about the family?

My grandmother used to stay depressed, crying, while watching people get sick or die on the "soap operas". I told her one-day, "Granny, they are actors. When they die on one show, they do not die in reality, they resurrect on another show with hundreds of thousands of dollars more money and you are left in poor health." She finally heard me and cut them off for good. Her demeanor changed dramatically.

Radio

Have you ever noticed that what you listen to in the mornings, often become the topics you talk about for a good part of your day? Your ear gates feed your mind, and your mind affects the way you feel. So if you are listening to someone angry, combative, racist, divisive or immoral, then your day will become ordered by the breakfast you eat. Have you noticed that word, breakfast? To "break" your "fast", what do you eat on? The first meal after sleeping through the night is your breakfast. What do you allow into your system after your mind, body and spirit has rested? Did you know that breakfast is the most important meal of the day? That most over-weight people do not eat breakfast or eat things that start their day off on the unbalanced, unhealthy side? Whatever you listen to in the morning (breakfast for your soul), either causes a balance or imbalance in your day.

According to the Word of God, "Faith comes by hearing", (Romans 10:17). Whatever you are is shaped by what you listen to on a daily basis, so protect your ear gates. It *does* matter what music you listen to. It *does* matter what message that music has in it. It is *not* just a song. It is not *just* a beat or a great guitarist. What are the words? Words have the power of death and life in them.

Books, Magazines and Internet

Education is important. The right education is critical. We are educated by everything we see and hear. There are books, tapes, magazines and Internet sites galore, that you can use to do research. At the touch of a button, we can get an education without ever leaving the quiet of our home. How far society has come, from traditional on-campus, in the library or classroom education. Technology is fascinating. Yet as instructive as technology is, it also has the potential to be destructive. In the wrong hands, most anything can be turned into a dangerous tool. A case in point is the tree of knowledge. It presented man with a choice, an option of good or evil. Left alone without proper guidance from his creator, man will often choose evil in some form. He will choose to satisfy himself, to serve himself, rather than others.

There are people in the world who spend their day writing material and creating websites for the sole purpose of enticing you to spend your life on pleasure, perversion and passions that destroy the very fiber or foundation of society. They are what I call cyberspace drug dealers. Their drug is as addictive as heroin and crack and also as destructive.

People

Everywhere in scripture we are warned about our association with certain people. Over and over, the children of

Israel found themselves estranged from God because they chose friendships with people who worshipped idols. First Corinthians 15:33 says, *"^{33}Do not be misled: "Bad company corrupts good character."* If you want to see what you look like, look at the people closest to you. You often advance or fail in life by the people with which you choose to associate yourself.

When you choose to fast, starve the flesh, you must make some very serious decisions about every one of the above areas. How important are they to you? Why? Because you have to evaluate each of those areas one by one and discover what is feeding your flesh and making you operate your life based on what you think, want or feel, as opposed to the will of God.

Is there something on television you need to stop watching for a period of time? Are there books, tapes, magazines or Internet sites that affect you negatively and cause you to ignore the voice of God in your ear? Ask yourself are there people you interact with who are critics, counselors, or so called friends, that call forth the "fool" in me and not the faithful, father, husband, wife, mother, Christ follower, role model, standard bearer or leader I'm called to be? If so, then decide that while I'm fasting, I must starve these areas from my life. It may be that I cannot go cold turkey, but one by one, I must do this to save me and see the me I was created to be. Starvation causes stomach pains and headaches initially. The body is used to coffee, caffeine, sugar etc. It rebels before it accepts. You will suffer withdrawals from your withdrawal, but then again, so does every addict. That is correct. We are trying to break an addiction to fleshly desires. It is the only way for you to see the supernatural life in which you were born again to operate.

The other side of "the soul man" is the spirit man. God is a spirit. He created us to operate by His spirit. He desires complete lordship of our lives. He is a jealous God. He does not like any other voice in our ears except His. Adam's fall came because he chose to follow another voice over the voice of his creator. When the created is controlled by the created, a fall is inevitable. The ongoing questions remain. Who is in charge? Is it the soulish (flesh) man? Or is it the spirit man? This is war!

> Liberty Savard, in her book, "*Producing the Promise (Keys of the Kingdom Trilogy Series*", spends considerable time dealing with the keys of binding and loosing (Matthew 16:19, 18:18), in prayer. In her introduction she writes, "*The binding and loosing keys of the Kingdom prayer principles – "Shattering Your Strongholds," appear to many to be just too simple. The unsurrendered soul of the born again Christian fights this simplicity, for the principles of the keys of the Kingdom allow no-room for self-preening (which the soul loves) for adhering to any religious regulations that would "make" you holy. Nor do the keys of the Kingdom prayer principles of surrendering everything to God allow for awards to be handed out for gritting-your-teeth acts of the self-will to overcome life's hardest things and turn them into worldly success.*
>
> *The soul has no interest in anything that does not recognize all it has been through and all it has accomplished on its own. It wants credit for pressing on despite all hurdles, for taking desperately heroic measures to overcome everything anyone has ever thrown at it. The soul also expects appropriate sympathy, praise, and compensation for having done so. To give God all of the credit is completely unappealing to the soul. To surrender its accumulated baggage and all rights to applause for having carried it so long is not acceptable to the*

unsurrendered soul, either. And terrifying to the soul is the fact that these keys can strip it of all of the games that keep it on the throne of your life." [9]

In other worlds, the soul will not give in easy. It wants to fight for its territory. It enjoys being in charge and will not surrender. It must be defeated and overcome by something stronger. As long as the soul is in charge, your spirit will never pray the prayers it needs to pray so it can cancel the agenda that will eventually lead to destruction. Paul said in Romans 7:21-25 {NLT}, *"[21]I have discovered this principle of life— that when I want to do what is right, I inevitably do what is wrong. [22]I love God's law with all my heart. [23]But there is another power within me that is at war with my mind. This power makes me a slave to the sin that is still within me. [24]Oh, what a miserable person I am! Who will free me from this life that is dominated by sin and death? [25]Thank God! The answer is in Jesus Christ our Lord. So you see how it is: In my mind I really want to obey God's law, but because of my sinful nature I am a slave to sin."*

Nine (9) New Testament Fasting Citings

There are nine observations I want you to consider from the New Testament concerning fasting. As you read them, allow each one to be inspiration to starve out the old man and begin refreshing the new (we will see how in chapter 4).

I. Matthew 4:2 – *"[2]After fasting forty days and forty nights, he was hungry."*

Mark 1:12-13 – *"[12]At once the Spirit sent him out into the desert, [13]and he was in the desert forty days, being*

---

[9] Liberty Savard, Producing the Promise-Keys of the Kingdom Trilogy Series, Bridge-Logos Publishers, Gainesville, Fl, 1999, xiii.

tempted by Satan. He was with the wild animals, and angels attended him."

As you can see, Jesus is fasting or has fasted. Note the Mark passage. It gives us the view of the scene that we possibly missed if we read the other two passages alone. Mark shares that Jesus is *in* the fast, being tempted by Satan. This suggests a fight *during* the fast, for what the Father is preparing you to do. If Satan can stop you early, he can prevent what you're being prepared to accomplish. He was there to stop Jesus from healing the sick, raising the dead, preaching the Kingdom, teaching disciples, and dying to save the world. He desires us to live with a longing for pleasures, accolades, titles, pride of accomplishments and credit for miraculous performances.

II. Matthew 9:14 – *"[14]Then John's disciples came and asked him, "How is it that we and the Pharisees fast, but your disciples do not fast?"*

Mark 2:18 – *"[18]Now John's disciples and the Pharisees were fasting. Some people came and asked Jesus, "How is it that John's disciples and the disciples of the Pharisees are fasting, but yours are not?"*

Notice that the disciples did not need to fast as long as Jesus was near or present. When He is gone or away or absent, then fasting is required. Whenever there is an absence of the presence of Jesus in your life style, you need a fast. Starve that area to death, until you see the appearance of Jesus show up.

III. Luke 2:37 – *"[37]and then was a widow until she was eighty-four. She never left the temple but worshiped night and day, fasting and praying."*

As you will read in a subsequent chapter, Anna got revelation from fasting (see chapter 7). Whenever you have trouble seeing, understanding principles of God, right from wrong, the vision for your house or for your ministry, fasting will open your eyes.

IV.   Luke 18:12 – *"¹²I fast twice a week and give a tenth of all I get."*

Here is a story about a religious man who did it all right, but had the wrong attitude. When you fast, give, pray or serve, it is unto the Lord, not for bragging rights about your super holiness. Fasting should make you humble, if you are doing it right. You fast because you are off track, so you can't brag about it. It was the Lord who redirected you. "I am what I am by the grace of God," should be your mentality.

V.   Mark 9-14-29 {KJV} – *"¹⁴And when he came to his disciples, he saw a great multitude about them, and the scribes questioning with them. ¹⁵And straightway all the people, when they beheld him, were greatly amazed, and running to him saluted him.*

¹⁶And he asked the scribes, What question ye with them?

¹⁷And one of the multitude answered and said, Master, I have brought unto thee my son, which hath a dumb spirit; ¹⁸And wheresoever he taketh him, he teareth him: and he foameth, and gnasheth with his teeth, and pineth away: and I spake to thy disciples that they should cast him out; and they could not.

¹⁹He answereth him, and saith, O faithless generation, how long shall I be with you? how long shall I suffer you? bring him unto me.

²⁰And they brought him unto him: and when he saw him, straightway the spirit tare him; and he fell on the ground, and wallowed foaming.

²¹And he asked his father, How long is it ago since this came unto him? And he said, Of a child. ²²And ofttimes it hath cast him into the fire, and into the waters, to destroy him: but if thou canst do any thing, have compassion on us, and help us.

²³Jesus said unto him, If thou canst believe, all things are possible to him that believeth.

²⁴And straightway the father of the child cried out, and said with tears, Lord, I believe; help thou mine unbelief.

²⁵When Jesus saw that the people came running together, he rebuked the foul spirit, saying unto him, Thou dumb and deaf spirit, I charge thee, come out of him, and enter no more into him

²⁶And the spirit cried, and rent him sore, and came out of him: and he was as one dead; insomuch that many said, He is dead. ²⁷But Jesus took him by the hand, and lifted him up; and he arose.

²⁸And when he was come into the house, his disciples asked him privately, Why could not we cast him out? ²⁹And he said unto them, This kind can come forth by nothing, but by prayer and fasting."

If you have not been able to break it by prayer alone, take your warfare to the next level. Satan is a flesh eater. He sees the soulish man and feeds off of him. He delights in our being stuck on ourselves. He enjoys us being stuck period. He knows that it renders us powerless. You cannot operate in the spirit realm against demonic powers without spiritual power.

You can't get that with physical food or by lifting free weights. You need to empty some stuff and grow up spiritually, so that you stop being bullied around by Satan.

VI.   Acts 13:2-3 – *"²While they were worshiping the Lord and fasting, the Holy Spirit said, "Set apart for me Barnabas and Saul for the work to which I have called them." ³So after they had fasted and prayed, they placed their hands on them and sent them off."*

Fasting is preparation for ministry. It prepares us for our journey. It puts us in the right frame of mind to do what God called us to do. It re-images us. Yet, that is what we see on the surface. We know that from reading Acts 13 alone. However, read chapter 12 and we note that apostles were being imprisoned and followers killed. Fasting, praying and worship must go together as a medicine of refreshment for difficult seasons. It strengthens us to press forward despite what we see.

VII.   Acts 14:22-23 – *"²²...strengthening the disciples and encouraging them to remain true to the faith."We must go through many hardships to enter the kingdom of God," they said. ²³Paul and Barnabas appointed elders for them in each church and, with prayer and fasting, committed them to the Lord, in whom they had put their trust."*

From the evidence of this commentary, we note that leadership requires you to be empowered to the highest level because you are vulnerable to the highest level of attack. Leaders who do not fast and pray are not leaders really strong enough to lead at all. They die in battle and their troops are headless-wanderers guided by whatever spirits that attach themselves to them.

VIII.   Acts 27:9 – *"⁹Much time had been lost, and sailing had already become dangerous because by now it was after the Fast. So Paul warned them,"*

Acts 27:33-35 – *"³³Just before dawn Paul urged them all to eat." For the last fourteen days," he said, "you have been in constant suspense and have gone without food—you haven't eaten anything. ³⁴Now I urge you to take some food. You need it to survive. Not one of you will lose a single hair from his head." ³⁵After he said this, he took some bread and gave thanks to God in front of them all. Then he broke it and began to eat."*

When you are on your way somewhere but cannot seem to see the destination clearly, or are in a storm and you know you are close and need a boost, fast. Fasting cancels fear. It builds faith in a foggy season. It gives you confidence to throw overboard, any excess weight that you think you need, but don't. What excess baggage are you carrying?

I read an article about the singer Aliyah. It was about the tragic story of a wonderful singer who demanded to take extra baggage on a flight, contrary of to the warning of an expert pilot, who cautioned that it would cause problems in the journey. She or her team, having the money and the fame obviously overruled and the flight took off but didn't land safely. Too much baggage caused deaths of not only the person whose bags they were but every other person on the plane.

IX.   II Corinthians 6:5 – *"⁵in beatings, imprisonments and riots; in hard work, sleepless nights and hunger;"*

II Corinthians 11:27 – *"²⁷I have labored and toiled and have often gone without sleep; I have known hunger and thirst and have often gone without food; I have been cold and naked."*

Some fasts are forced because of travel, poverty or famine. I contend that it is great to practice fasting, because if you are ever faced with a time you *have* to do without, you will be prepared, because you have disciplined yourself for any battle. Fasting during tough financial seasons is wise. You save money. You eat less and need less, therefore you go fewer places. In short, you have less of a need for entertainment by the world, therefore you spend less money.

God Sees Dead People

God is searching for dead people. People who are dead to sin, dead to their way of thinking, wanting and feeling, but alive to Him are the ones to whom He is giving revelation. Let us close this chapter with why dead people are so attractive to God.

1. They move when they are told.

2. They never talk back.

3. They cannot ever be offended – spit on them, talk about them, ignore them, don't call their names out in appreciation, don't recognize them.

4. They can be left in the dark till the last minute and are always ready to go.

5. They never complain about where they're going, or how long they have to be there.

6. They never concern themselves about who they have to be in the company of, or room with.

7. They wear what you tell them and stay in place when you place them.

8. They never change their expression no matter the circumstances.

9. There is no hidden agenda with them; you can always check them out. What you see is what you get.

10. They never rise up because of compliments: pride, ego.

11. Material things are insignificant, they have them or they do not, and with or without them, they are the same person.

Well, let's see what chapter 5 has to offer. Get ready to eat all you can. It's time to feed the spirit man.

5
Eat All You Can-
Building Up the Spirit Man

> *Joel 1:14 -Declare a holy fast; call a sacred assembly. Summon the elders and all who live in the land to the house of the LORD your God, and cry out to the LORD.*

The word is out that fasting is just about giving up food. Let me go on record as saying, that fasting is not really all about giving up food. This is at the root of fasting, but it is not the end result. In actuality, you can eat until your heart is content while you are on a fast. However, there is a twist. The twist is simply this, you can eat all you want, but you must eat the right food. Fasting is really a food substitution lifestyle. It is not a food cancellation lifestyle. It means that we replace one food with another. We give up one food for another for the purpose of greater nourishment.

Daniel 10:2-3 says, *"[2]At that time I, Daniel, mourned for three weeks. [3]I ate no choice food; no meat or wine touched my lips; and I used no lotions at all until the three weeks were over."* He says in essence that he feasted off of the presence of God, alone. He allowed God to make him fat. When you fast, you under nourish the soulish man but you build up the spirit man. The soulish man gets smaller and smaller during a fast, while the spirit man grows up. The key ingredient to the fast is not about what you are not eating, but what you are eating. You must grow up the spirit man so that it reaches maturity, while starving the flesh.

In order to grow the spirit man up to maturity, we must be on a proper eating schedule, having the right food on the menu, while decreasing the intake of things that steal our ability to be dominators in the earth. I starve my will, and feed His will for my life, until His will is greater than mine. If I cannot overcome a piece of pie, then I will never be able to say no to tobacco. If I cannot say no to a piece of fried food, I cannot say no to a sexual offer that is outside of my marriage. The no to physical food is to build up my strength to fight sins influence in my life. This is only the beginning. I still need something to replace the food I am giving up. I need to eat. When I eat I need meals that make me better. So now my meals are substituted by food from the Word of God

Ultimately, it is not the food; it is His lordship I am after. My one desire is to be able to hear His directions clearly so that I make fewer to no errors in my daily walk. I want to experience Ephesians 3:20, *"[20]Now to him who is able to do immeasurably more than all we ask or imagine, according to his power that is at work within us."* I am after experiencing what Paul was feeling when he wrote Philippians 3:10, *"[10]I want to know Christ and the power of his resurrection and the fellowship of sharing in his sufferings, becoming like him in his death."*

Jesus said something that cost Him his life. He said, "Not my will but thine be done". This is proof that He crucified His flesh, long before we saw that flesh die on the cross. No wonder it is said that no one took His life – He gave it, not in court, but in the garden where he prayed, "never the less". He said, "I am a dead man now." Paul said it this way, "Not I that live, but Christ (the anointed one and His anointing) lives in me." Galatians 2:20 says, *"[20]I have been crucified with Christ and I no longer live, but Christ lives in me. The life I live in the body, I live by faith in the Son of God, who loved me and gave himself for me."* These two men exemplify what mature Christianity looks like. We need to know what it looks like so we have a target at which to aim.

What Mature Christians Look Like

Rick Warren, in his book, The Purpose Driven Life, offers us this, *"We are commanded to think the same way that Christ Jesus thought. There are two parts to doing this. The first half of this mental shift is to stop thinking immature thoughts, which are self-centered and self-seeking. The Bible says, Stop thinking like children. In regard to evil be infants, but in your thinking be adults. Babies by nature are completely selfish. They think only of themselves and their own needs. They are incapable of giving; they can only receive. That is immature thinking. Unfortunately, many people never grow beyond that kind of thinking. The Bible says that selfish thinking is the source of sinful behavior: Those who live following their sinful selves think only about things that their sinful selves want. The second half of thinking like Jesus is to start thinking maturely, which focuses on others, not yourself. In his great chapter on what real love is; Paul concluded that thinking of others is the mark of maturity: When I was a child I talked like a child, I thought like a child, I reasoned like a child. When I became a man, I put childish thinking behind me."* [10]

---

[10] Rick Warren, *The Purpose Driven Life*, Zondervan, Grand Rapids MI, 2002, pg 182-183.

While knowledge is one measurement of maturity, it isn't the whole story. The Christian life is far more than creeds and convictions; it includes conduct and character. Our deeds must be consistent with our creeds. Our beliefs must be backed up with Christ-like behavior.

Undoubtedly, the best picture to look at for modeling purposes is the life of Jesus and the life of the Apostle Paul. Paul was a disciple maker. He was a man on a mission to grow believers up from childhood to maturity. We will investigate several scriptures to help portray the maturity that needs to be reached, and then I will offer you my personal path that I found by fasting the right way. As we will learn in chapters to come, a fast must be done right. Many people who call themselves fasting are just on a starvation diet. Remember, it is not just what you do not eat; it is what you *are* eating that matters as well.

Every Christian should have as a goal, to grow up to maturity. There are simple stages that we go through as human beings: newborn, child-hood, adolescence (teens) and adult (young adult, middle age, elder). As a newborn and child, you are being taught to talk, walk, and know right from wrong, potty training, basic manners and discipline. At the adolescent stage your learning increases. You move from the basics to more legal things because in the future, failure to abide by rules has criminal ramifications (institutionalization-incarceration-prison). This stage is the stage where responsibilities are given as well. One begins to be given assignments, tasks to achieve (running errands, cleaning up your room, washing dishes and even babysitting). At this stage, we are in preparation or training for our future roles as reproducers of the population, which is the role of those, not just the cared for or provided for, but those doing the providing.

The next stage is adulthood. In the *young* adulthood stage, we begin to educate ourselves on what we plan to do with the rest of our lives. By educating *ourselves*, I do not mean we are no longer taught by others. I mean simply, that we begin to make choices about the remainder of our lives, and on what areas we will be focusing most our attention. Our eyes begin to change from focusing from the "game" stage, to the "career" stage. It is in this stage, if we have received proper training, and accepted it, that we begin being available for wedding ourselves to another. In this stage, we are mentoring those behind us who are seeking knowledge as we once were. When we find that person who we *know* God has made to bring us to completion, we then wed ourselves to them, becoming one with them. This union begins again the cycle from whence we started.

It is important to note how critical nourishment is to every step of the journey. Our health depends upon our eating habits. Junk food will eventually produce a broken down body. Bad health is the product of three things in general: first, there are some things genetically handed down; second, poor diet, (which includes the lack of enough water and everything else the fast food industry has greatly contributed to); finally, the lack of proper exercising.

When you apply the above to your spiritual life, you can see just where you are on the life cycle. Are you a newborn? Are you still in childhood? Are others still feeding you baby food? Are you not yet eating on your own or are you told when to eat? Are you always crying when things go wrong, not knowing how to correct problems? Do you not know how to control your bowel movements? Still stinking up public places because you do not know to go to private areas and flush out foul indwellings (I do not mean physically)?

Are you at adolescence? Are you living a sneaky life? Are you still learning some right from wrong? Or do you know, but are trying to get away with what you can? Exploring? Wondering should you be real, responsible, disciplined, study hard or someone who does just enough to get by? Are games, girls or guys still more important than goals guidelines and gifts you have inside of you?

Most Christians live their lives like they are dieting. I need to lose a *little* weight. I know I am too fat to get in my wedding dress or bathing suit. Or my doctor said I need to take off a few pounds for health reasons, so I diet for a while, lose the weight, but nothing is broken. I do not do it for life, but for an event. I want to look good for an event. I do it for other's approval or to please *me* for a while. But because nothing is broken, old habits resurface, and I crave that which I stopped doing for a while. Often the end result is that I end up returning to it. It is the dog retuning to its own vomit. I make up for lost time and I end up being worse than I was before. Sound familiar?

This is why every Christian needs a picture of who they were born to be at the beginning of this journey, so that we eat according to our destiny, not our desires. We feed and train according to that which we were designed by God to become. If in fact, we did not do this early in our Christian walk, it is not too late. This is where fasting comes in to play. It gives us a chance to be reborn, to clean out the old, in order to purify us. Now we can go back and paint the look-a-like portrait of Jesus in us, so we know what we are to look like. After this painting, then comes the meal preparation, so we build healthy Christian lives. Did you know many Christians do not read the bible? Well, then that would explain why the world has become so dysfunctional. Malnutrition in the church is the leading cause of world disorder. The Earth is groaning waiting for the sons of God to be revealed (Romans 8:19-22). I know what, you are saying, "If I only knew who I was supposed to be. If I knew who I was I could act the part." Well, today is your birthday. You are getting ready to enjoy a wonderful gift. It is your party. It is your day to celebrate your birth into the mature realm. Today we take a peek at what it looks like, so you can live out your purpose for existence.

Every person on planet earth was born to rule/dominate/lead, according to Genesis chapters 1 and 2. We were born to "be fruitful, multiply, replenish the earth…to have dominion." There is "genius" in our genes. Our DNA has divinity in it. We are, indeed a special breed. There are some names we are called in the New Testament that I believe you should know about. They are names that you should have in mind while you are fasting. Your goal is to see yourself with each of these characteristics as a part of your persona.

Ambassador – II Corinthians 5:20 – *"[20]We are therefore Christ's ambassadors, as though God were making his appeal through us. We implore you on Christ's behalf: Be reconciled to God."*

An ambassador is a diplomat of the highest rank, accredited by government, as representative in residence to another – a diplomatic agent of the highest rank accredited to a foreign government or the sovereign as the resident representative of his or her own government, or appointed for a special and often temporary diplomatic assignment.[11] We are here in "time", on assignment for the King, to rule in the region called the earth. I believe we were called to keep watch over the work and workers of iniquity. We were assigned to keep him locked down and living beneath his former privileges. He was an arch (leader) angel and his demeanor demoted him. "Self" stole his birthright. Pride imprisoned him. We were created to remind him of who he was and have him suffer and agonize at the choice he made, to be worshipped rather than to worship. When we praise and worship God, it is stoking the flames of hell, infuriating its chief inhabitant.

Every person born here is on assignment to do just that. A problem occurred however. Genesis 3:1 – says "The serpent was craftier than all of the wild animals…" suggesting that when man walks on the wild side, he is vulnerable to trickery. When man walks in unrestraint, refusing to be God-controlled, disciplined, vision-focused, he is subject to living a fallen life.

---

[11] *Merriam-Webster Online Dictionary* Merriam-Webster, Incorporated, 2005

Adam made a choice to listen to voices that were contrary to his creator, and the rest is history. Thereby, man had to be given a new assignment. Correct yourself! Protect yourself by repentance! Recover lost brothers and sisters to the father! These assignments never cease. This is the job of the ambassador. Discover where you came from. Learn everything possible about your home and the principles, laws, operations of it, as well as the desires of the King. Know that where you are, you represent King and country in everything you say and do. You never move by your emotions. Galatians 2:20 says, *"[20]I have been crucified with Christ and I no longer live, but Christ lives in me. The life I live in the body, I live by faith in the Son of God, who loved me and gave himself for me."* Your every decision is based upon information you get from the King. **You are Him**, not you. Your orders are bigger than your feelings. What you are there for is worth more than you are aware. It is important for you to see what the King sees if you can. But in the event that you do not, do what he says without thinking about it. He knows the end result, which you sometimes have to wait and see.

Bride of Christ – Revelation 19:7 – *"[7]Let us rejoice and be glad and give him glory! For the wedding of the Lamb has come, and his bride has made herself ready."*

This biblical terminology sounds strange to the male Christian; however, we have no problems when the bible refers to us all as "sons". Jesus is the first-born of many "sons". The church is the body of Christ. The body must eat properly to live. Its bread and meat is the word. It cannot live off of anything worldly. A supernatural body needs supernatural food. We *are* the Church, the body or the *bride* of Christ; the bride of the perfect one. He cannot marry himself to a whore. The church is not a building where people come. The church is a people who gather in a building. I am the church. You are the church my dear friend. Now the question is this, are we worthy to be married to the Son of God? Will His Daddy permit His perfect Son to be married to us? Are we the helpmeet He's looking for? What are you eating that will make Him admire you enough for matrimony? Are you fat (overweight with the world or fat, just right with the word or the anointing? Isaiah 10:27 – *"²⁷In that day their burden will be lifted from your shoulders, their yoke from your neck; the yoke will be broken because you have grown so fat."*

God's Temple – I Corinthians 3:16 – *"¹⁶Don't you know that you yourselves are God's temple and that God's Spirit lives in you?"*

You are the temple of God. He is not looking for a brick and mortar building in which He can worship. He is looking for *you* to host Him. You are the building He created for worship. You house His Spirit. In you resides every gift, every fruit waiting to bestow on someone. In you is the breath of life waiting to be breathed on someone. You are the seed that will produce a harvest of righteousness in the earth. What you put in your body will either add to or steal from the anointing (the power to break yokes, remove burdens and assist people to their divinely designed destiny). If you are not committed to marrying the anointed one, you will involve yourself with any kind of spirits, and on the wedding day, there will not be enough oil for you to see the aisle that leads to the altar.

Holy Priesthood – I Peter 2:4-5, *"⁴As you come to him, the living Stone—rejected by men but chosen by God and precious to him— ⁵you also, like living stones, are being built into a spiritual house to be a holy priesthood, offering spiritual sacrifices acceptable to God through Jesus Christ."*

You were born to be a priest. Not in the sense that you know it, as in Catholicism, but in the sense that it is referred to in the Old Testament. The priests sacrificed offerings for the sins of others. That is supposed to be recognized as a mature position. Ezekiel 22:30 says, *"³⁰ "I looked for a man among them who would build up the wall and stand before me in the gap on behalf of the land so I would not have to destroy it, but I found none."* Were there no mature men anywhere who would be priests for their nation? Jeremiah 8:22 says, *"²² Is there no balm in Gilead? Is there no physician there? Why then is there no healing for the wound of my people?"* Mature Christians take less time trying to fix their sins. The seeing of sin in your life, and delaying to rid yourself of it, is for children or adolescents, not for grow ups. When you reach the stage of maturity you become a model for others. It says that you are a teacher. You have become a helper. I have been there. Here is help to escape the world and arrive at that place. It is sometimes tough arriving and staying there without ever going back to adolescence. It helps seeing your picture. Getting a view of the new you is good.

Salt of the Earth – Matthew 5:13 – *"¹³"You are the salt of the earth. But if the salt loses its saltiness, how can it be made salty again? It is no longer good for anything, except to be thrown out and trampled by men."*

John Koessler, writes, *"Jesus' reference to salt would also have been familiar to the disciples because it was used by the rabbis, who compared the Torah, the first five books of the Old Testament, to salt, and said, "the world cannot survive without salt." Jesus was saying, in effect, "You are the living Torah to those around you."*[12] Wow! You are the Genesis, the beginning of peoples' life. They begin to see who they were made to be by watching you. You are the Exodus, the Moses that leads them out of bondage, whatever that bondage is they may be in. You are their Levite, their Leviticus, and the

---

[12] John Koessler, *Names of the Believers*, Moody Press, Chicago, IL 1997, pg 10

standard by which they live. I repeat, the only God they have seen is in you. You are the revelation of the many guiding principles for living the God kind of life. You are their Numbers, you separate them from the evil Korah's and misguided Miriam's, and the small minded people they see in the church. You help them to see their promised land. You are Deuteronomy, the Law of God walking. You are the living epistle. You represent the best God has to offer. They see in you a person who says, "I will not quit on you until you reach your destiny. I will present the choice before you and spell out the benefits and consequences, blessings or curses". You are their food that helps them experience blessings.

Servant – I Corinthians 4:1 – *"¹So then, men ought to regard us as servants of Christ and as those entrusted with the secret things of God."*

This word has the appearance of unworthiness. It is often a title undesirably worn. Who wants to be known as a servant? Why would anyone want to get to this place? Everything we know about the word says, lesser, little person, lowest, last, least, forgotten, nobody, stepped on and over. Yet, I list it last because, "the last shall be first." The way up is down. The way down is to be "uppity". I have a philosophy. If you are too big to serve, you are too big. He that desires to sit on the throne must first learn to bow before it. In other words, serve your way to leadership.

Jesus said in Matthew 23:11, *"¹¹The greatest among you will be your servant."* No matter what the world thinks of you, serve. No matter what title is bestowed upon you, that title does not ever relinquish you from serving. When Bishop Wellington Boone walked down the aisle of my son in ministry's church to give some remarks at a Thanksgiving Service in 2006, it was a life breaking surprise what happened next. Spontaneously, he removed his Bishop's ring (of which he called his last and favorite) placed it on my finger and spoke over my life blessing and explanation of the office I was called to walk in. I still wipe my face, or at least get choked up at times, when telling that story. I tell it for this reason, when I returned to the pulpit I was assigned to as Senior Pastor, I said these words to the people, "This ring is not for bragging rights. It is a privilege to wear it, but it does not make me more privileged than you. It is a signet that I have been called lower, deeper into serving." I also said to them that as I was called to greater service so would our ministry be. I could not make that statement with integrity without dying to my flesh. Still, to this day my flesh wants to rise for recognition, and I have to make sure it submits to the spirit of Christ in me. Fasting is the only way to do that.

The question that lingers must be this, "How will what you do on a daily basis glorify God?" Colossians 3:1-17 helps us see our pathway to the mature life. The end result is to see everything as something you do for Christ.

> Colossians 3:1-17 – "*[1] Since, then, you have been raised with Christ, set your hearts on things above, where Christ is seated at the right hand of God. [2] Set your minds on things above, not on earthly things. [3] For you died, and your life is now hidden with Christ in God. [4] When Christ, who is your life, appears, then you also will appear with him in glory.*
>
> *[5] Put to death, therefore, whatever belongs to your earthly nature: sexual immorality, impurity, lust, evil desires and greed, which is idolatry. [6] Because of these, the wrath of God is coming. [7] You used to walk in these ways, in the life you once lived. [8] But now you must rid yourselves of all such things as these: anger, rage, malice, slander, and filthy language from your lips. [9] Do not lie to each other, since you have taken off your old self with its practices*

¹⁰and have put on the new self, which is being renewed in knowledge in the image of its Creator. ¹¹Here there is no Greek or Jew, circumcised or uncircumcised, barbarian, Scythian, slave or free, but Christ is all, and is in all.

¹²Therefore, as God's chosen people, holy and dearly loved, clothe yourselves with compassion, kindness, humility, gentleness and patience. ¹³Bear with each other and forgive whatever grievances you may have against one another. Forgive as the Lord forgave you. ¹⁴And over all these virtues put on love, which binds them all together in perfect unity.

¹⁵Let the peace of Christ rule in your hearts, since as members of one body you were called to peace. And be thankful. ¹⁶Let the word of Christ dwell in you richly as you teach and admonish one another with all wisdom, and as you sing psalms, hymns and spiritual songs with gratitude in your hearts to God. ¹⁷And whatever you do, whether in word or deed, do it all in the name of the Lord Jesus, giving thanks to God the Father through him."

If you and I are going to live this kind of life and please God, then our eating habits will have to be designed and kept. As a child I ate according to my taste buds. If I didn't like it, I didn't eat it. Therefore I never ate spinach, carrots, cauliflower or peas unless under PG (parental guidance). Without a parent at the table, I used the closest garbage can to consume my dislikes. Our garbage can was *really healthy*. When I became a man, I began to study health and become conscious of what those vegetables did *for* me. I began to eat based upon my needs and not my wants. People don't take medicine because they want to. They do it because they feel a need. Often, with children, it must be forced, but adults (mature people) do it willfully, because they know the consequences of not taking it. The same is so with the Word of God. You also must eat healthy spiritually. You cannot live off of "fast-food" Word. You need a healthy balanced meal. You need it prepared right and not so much gravy that you miss the meat (so much emotion that the message gets lost). Undernourishment will be the result of this kind of diet. I "feel good" is not the place to be after every worship experience. After some services you should feel like you have had surgery or been challenged or convicted.

Building on the Basic Foundation

Every fast needs to call us back to basics. If the foundation is flawed then the building is in trouble. It may look good, but it will fall. Too many Christians today are looking good on the outside but lacking the foundation of integrity and character. We are experiencing a fall in the body of Christ because we learned the art of building mega ministries without learning that which keeps them standing. We learned how to attract people, build buildings, raise money, market ourselves and ministry, preach to a moving message to a crowd and run a business. Yet we forgot the foundation, Christ and Him crucified (in me and with me). I try to instill one main principle in my sons and daughters in the faith, which I needed to hear when I began in ministry, "character before communication". Because it is too often not stressed, many leaders are falling. Even when it is stressed early, it must be reinforced later. The foundation must continue to be strengthened. The higher you go the more fasting and praying you need to do. Here is a brief menu of foundational foods you will need for every fast. Whatever else you add (supplements) will be based upon your needs in a particular area. II Peter 1:5 says "add to your faith…" So build on these four basic cornerstones, so that your life and ministry will not just have outer beauty, but inner stability.

Faith
Hebrew 11:6 – *"⁶And without faith it is impossible to please God, because anyone who comes to him must believe that he exists and that he rewards those who earnestly seek him."*

II Peter 1:5 – *"⁵For this very reason, make every effort to add to your faith goodness; and to goodness, knowledge..."* Add to your faith by studying His names during your fast. Gain confidence in His *"ableness"*, His faithfulness. (Study Abraham and Daniel)

Love
I Corinthians 13:1-8 – *"¹If I speak in the tongues of men and of angels, but have not love, I am only a resounding gong or a clanging cymbal. ²If I have the gift of prophecy and can fathom all mysteries and all knowledge, and if I have a faith that can move mountains, but have not love, I am nothing. ³If I give all I possess to the poor and surrender my body to the flames, but have not love, I gain nothing.*

⁴Love is patient, love is kind. It does not envy, it does not boast, it is not proud. ⁵It is not rude, it is not self-seeking, it is not easily angered, it keeps no record of wrongs. ⁶Love does not delight in evil but rejoices with the truth. ⁷It always protects, always trusts, always hopes, always perseveres.

⁸Love never fails. But where there are prophecies, they will cease; where there are tongues, they will be stilled; where there is knowledge, it will pass away."

Galatians 5:5-6 says faith works by love. I John 4 and 5 tell us much about love. God is love – you cannot be a child of love and still hate, be constantly angry, causing disharmony or strife (fighting).

Gifts

Ephesians 4:11-14 – *"[11]It was he who gave some to be apostles, some to be prophets, some to be evangelists, and some to be pastors and teachers, [12]to prepare God's people for works of service, so that the body of Christ may be built up [13]until we all reach unity in the faith and in the knowledge of the Son of God and become mature, attaining to the whole measure of the fullness of Christ.*

[14]Then we will no longer be infants, tossed back and forth by the waves, and blown here and there by every wind of teaching and by the cunning and craftiness of men in their deceitful scheming."

I Corinthians 12:4-11 – *"[4]There are different kinds of gifts, but the same Spirit. [5]There are different kinds of service, but the same Lord. [6]There are different kinds of working, but the same God works all of them in all men.*

[7]Now to each one the manifestation of the Spirit is given for the common good. [8]To one there is given through the Spirit the message of wisdom, to another the message of knowledge by means

of the same Spirit, [9]to another faith by the same Spirit, to another gifts of healing by that one Spirit, [10]to another miraculous powers, to another prophecy, to another distinguishing between spirits, to another speaking in different kinds of tongues, and to still another the interpretation of tongues [11]All these are the work of one and the same Spirit, and he gives them to each one, just as he determines."

I Corinthians 12:25-26 – *"[25]so that there should be no division in the body, but that its parts should have equal concern for each other. [26]If one part suffers, every part suffers with it; if one part is honored, every part rejoices with it."*

I must never forget that I have been given gifts and that I am a gift. I cannot brag on what I have. It is not mine. I can only boast on the one who gave it to me. If I brag on me, I invalidate myself, and strip me of the right to have what I have been given. I become *god*. I become the object of my own worship. I become Satan, and deserve his plight. I render myself "anti" Christian – anti- Christ-like, to be ruled not to rule.

Prayer
John 17 – Pray for yourself, pray for other disciples in the body, pray for unbelievers to be joined to the body of Christ..

Matthew 6:9-13 is Jesus' Model Prayer
"[9]"This, then, is how you should pray: " 'Our Father in heaven, hallowed be your name,

[10]your kingdom come, your will be done on earth as it is in heaven.
[11]Give us today our daily bread.

¹²Forgive us our debts, as we also have forgiven our debtors

¹³And lead us not into temptation, but deliver us from the evil one'

Jude 1:20 – *"²⁰But you, dear friends, build yourselves up in your most holy faith and pray in the Holy Spirit."* Pray in the Holy Spirit daily and often. Finish every session with I believe I received it. Do not let *any* day go by without building yourself up.

Study different prayers in the Bible. Read the word and pray what you read. Learn to say back to God what He says to you.

So you see, eating is essential in fasting. So get yourself ready to eat, but make sure you put the right food on the menu. Get ready to build that spiritual giant in you and watch that flesh man become a voice so quiet and small, that you cannot hear it. Make him fear to speak, because he knows laughter will erupt.

Now, get ready. We are moving to some touchy territory. Many people who are young in the faith cannot stand up and face what lies ahead. Put your seat belt on, there will be turbulence. **Breaking Strongholds and Canceling Generational Curses** is next.

6
Breaking Strongholds and Canceling Generational Curses

> Nehemiah 9:1-3 – *"¹On the twenty-fourth day of the same month, the Israelites gathered together, fasting and wearing sackcloth and having dust on their heads. ²Those of Israelite descent had separated themselves from all foreigners. They stood in their places and confessed their sins and the wickedness of their fathers. ³They stood where they were and read from the Book of the Law of the LORD their God for a quarter of the day, and spent another quarter in confession and in worshiping the LORD their God."*

There is a difference between a curse and a stronghold. They both have devastating potential. A stronghold is defined as, "a strong or well - fortified place; a fortress; a secure retreat or abode." [13] A plan dominated by a particular group or marked by a particular characteristic; a plan of protection; a place of hiding." [14] It is a place where, on the one hand you are so secure that intruders cannot easily come in, and on the other, if held prisoner, you cannot easily escape.

---

[13] The New Century Dictionary. Appleton Century Company, New York, NY, 1948, pg 1870

[14] Neil Anderson, *Victory Over The Darkness*, Regal Books, Ventura, CA, 2000 pg 90

It could be labeled as *anything* on which a person relies. In the Old Testament, God is seen as our stronghold. Amos 3:10 says, *"¹⁰"They do not know how to do right," declares the LORD, "who hoard plunder and loot in their fortresses.""* Then, Zechariah 9:12 says, *"¹²Return to your fortress, O prisoners of hope; even now I announce that I will restore twice as much to you."* Obviously, we are much better off on the Old Testament side of this understanding. When we come to the New Testament, 2 Corinthians 10:5 {KJV} introduces us to the stronghold on the other side. It says, *"⁵Casting down imaginations, and every high thing that exalteth itself against the knowledge of God, and bringing into captivity every thought to the obedience of Christ"*. Anything that positions itself to guard us from the knowledge of God is positioned to blind us and lead us to death and destruction. Our knowledge of God is our food for life, that which teaches us who we are, why we are here, and where we are going. Anything that would obscure that vision is dangerous to our health and must be destroyed.

One of the definitions in Vines' Concise Dictionary of the Bible says that when a curse is on something, it is devoted to destruction[15]. A curse emanates from some sinful act or actions. The bible however, shows us how they can connect to one another. When sin enters and is not broken, it becomes a stronghold in a person's life. It then has the capability of removing God's hand of blessing or favor; protection or prosperity (peace, provisions etc.). An unbroken stronghold in a person's life can bring about a curse. The tragedy is that the curse can be inherited, passed down to generations (Exodus 20:5, which says, *"⁵You shall not bow down to them or worship them; for I, the LORD your God, am a jealous God, punishing the children for the sin of the fathers to the third and fourth generation of those who hate me."*

---

[15] Vine's Complete Expository Dictionary of Old and New Testament Words ,1984, 1996, Thomas Nelson, Inc., Nashville, TN, pg 53

Nehemiah 9:1-3 offers to us both an understanding of how Israel got into the uncomfortable place in which they found themselves, as well as a plan of escape. It says,

> *"²Those of Israelite descent had separated themselves from all foreigners. They stood in their places and confessed their sins and the wickedness of their fathers. ³They stood where they were and read from the Book of the Law of the LORD their God for a quarter of the day, and spent another quarter in confession and in worshiping the LORD their God."*

As we travel through this chapter, it will call for you to take a close look at some people you may love and respect dearly, not so you will stop loving them, but so you can shake off any seen or unseen thing that you have inherited.

When the bible calls the Word of God a "two edged sword", it suggests to us that it kills and builds. It kills or destroys the wrong on one hand, and on the other, it builds us up to maturity. It cuts away to create room for character to be built. Then it fills the empty crevices with fresh manna (Word), so that it heals, and we grow, into a strong vital part of the body. This is why the Word is so important during a fast. You cannot overcome strongholds or break curses without fasting. Desire must be destroyed by spiritual warfare. Many times, people will think things are over in their lives because they have gone to therapists and treatment centers, or through programs. I am not here to demean or downplay the role that persons and programs play. However, some of them promote the constant confession of the problem, rather than confessing the answer or solution. I do not want you to confess for the rest of your life, that you are an alcoholic, drug addict, child abuser, homosexual, thief, sex offender, pornography addict, smoker, gambler, etc. At some point, you must get past the confession of your sins and move to the profession of your faith. God is a deliver. God is a healer. He can and will make you brand new. He truly *is* in the rehabilitation, restoration and reconciliation business, unlike some of our worldly institutions. Your only hope for true, lasting freedom is in Him. It is the reason He sent His son. My tears, if you could see them, flow for you. I feel your future. I know what it's like to be imprisoned by the enemy. To be filled with potential, but held captive by unseen curses and invited strongholds, then imprisoned by pride, which leads to destruction. I know what it's like to feel alone and no one to turn to because you fear trusting anyone to help you take steps towards the pathway to wholeness, holiness and a life of understood and pursued purpose. This, by the way, is the life that will experience total fulfillment. Any other kind of life is filled with superficiality. We settle for imitations until we have had a taste of, or experience with, the real thing. Then we realize imitations are insufficient, at least for us. Every young boy or girl is smitten by puppy love. They think they know exactly what love is. It is a feeling I have never had. "She kissed me.' "He told me he loved me." "He wants me to have his baby." It's sex." It's having enough money." "He can buy the things I never had." All of these things may be involved in an earthly relationship that has true love, but in and of themselves, they do not define love. Love can only be defined or described when you understand its origin. Everything else is cheap imitation. Until you have experienced true, God-kind of love, you will settle for the imitation. Once you see true love in motion, nothing less than that will satisfy you. My friend, do not settle for anything else but the life God promises you.

The Perfecting Pathway: 12 Crossroads

The perfecting pathway is labeled the "Fasted Life", but has many intercessions: Analysis; Awareness; Ashamed; Agitated; Arrested; Aloof; Abortive; Alive; Aggressive; Anointed; and Appointed. These intercessions are intersections along the road to the life God designed for you and me. I misspelled intersection and wrote intercession and got a revelation that this is exactly what each crossroad is. It is an intercession. It is a standing in the gap for each crossroad you have yet to face in the future. It is a time of praying for the strength to proceed to that next place along the path of your "assignment", so that you can begin, without fear of enemy embarrassment, to fulfilling your purpose in the earth. Aren't you weary yet of wearing the imitation when the genuine is available?

Analysis

The one thing about the genuine you, is that it will take time and effort. The work is worth it. Let's get started. There are two passages of scriptures that are important to read here.

> Lamentations 3:40-42, *"[40]Let us examine our ways and test them, and let us return to the LORD. [41]Let us lift up our hearts and our hands to God in heaven, and say: [42]"We have sinned and rebelled and you have not forgiven."*

> II Corinthians 13:5 – *"[5]Examine yourselves to see whether you are in the faith; test yourselves. Do you not realize that Christ Jesus is in you—unless, of course, you fail the test?"*

Both of these scriptures challenge us to take a good look at ourselves to see whether there is anything in us that needs re-imaging. Do we have anything in our lives working against us in the form of a curse or stronghold? Do you know your ancestry? What were your parents, grandparents and great-grandparents sins, hurts or secrets? Do you see any of *their* bad habits (strongholds) in *your* life? You cannot fix what you will not face. It is time to identify *everything* that is the source of incarcerating your true identity. Face your demons. What areas do you need help in? Need a minute? Get your journal out. Don't have one? Get one now! Okay, please! Make some notes, in code, if you have to, but write them down. Write dates, situations, people, places, anything that you can use to remember. This is not an exercise to hurt you, but to help you destroy the venom of your past so that it ceases to poison you, so that one day you can use it to help someone else. You need to know the root of why you do what you do. Why you drink, smoke, internet search, lie, steal, cheat, gamble, argue, are easily angered, abusive, have marriage issues, shut down and refuse to talk to anyone, do not love on your wife, children, see women as sex objects, or men as money? Why do you spend money so recklessly? Why do you have such a need to be recognized? Why do you procrastinate? Why do you sleep with anyone who is nice to you? Why are you attracted to the same sex? Why do you have extramarital affairs? Why are sports more important than your family, or more important than God? Are you an old frustrated ex-athlete? Why is poverty an option for you? Why do you not finish things you start?

Awareness

In Dr. Henry Malone's book, *Shadow Boxing*, he writes, "The schemes of the demonic realm affect your life. Have you ever felt as if a cloud was hanging over your head or a dark shadow was following you? Maybe it seemed as if there was an invisible barrier keeping you from what you really want to do or become. If so, it's time to sharpen your spiritual sight and realize there is more in this life than what can be seen! For example, if you are a Christian, chances are you have at some time in your life experienced an attack or a temptation from Satan. In your heart, you knew what was happening. You could "see" it with your spiritual eyes. But you may not have understood how to withstand it, or why that particular thing happened on that particular day. Without a proper understanding of the spiritual world, you were engaged in a fight for which you had not been trained."[16]

---

[16] Henry Malone, *Shadow Boxing*, Vision Life Publications, Irving TX, 1999, pg 45

Dr. Malone helps us to understand how Satan intrudes upon our lives with intent to affect the outcome of God's purpose for us. His desire is to keep us off balance, in emotional turmoil, with what Luke 13 says about the daughter of Abraham, who was bent over because of a *"spirit of infirmity"*. Dr. Malone shares five (5) primary strategies Satan uses to defeat us, of which we need to be aware.

Strategy 1: Lies and deception, where he tells the story of a woman angry with God because she said God let her father molest her. He offered to the lady that God was a man of His word and could not lie. Because her ancestors didn't love God enough to serve Him and worship Him, rather loving sin and self; their sins got visited to the third and fourth generation. You my friend, should decide today to be a curse breaker in your family lineage. Satan tried to deceive this woman to believe, that what happened to her was God's fault.

Strategy 2: Accusations and Condemnation in which Satan tries to convince us, that because of failures in our past, we are no good, a failure, unworthy to be loved, stupid, not smart enough. Years ago, I had an elderly woman in our church that came in to serve as a secretary. She used to say, after failing in an attempt to accomplish something, "I'm so dumb." I listened to it for a while, respecting her age. Then one day I had heard that statement made enough. I said, "Listen Mrs. Davis, do not say that one more time, please. You are not dumb because you made an error, or forgot something. You are who God says you are only." She has gone home to be with the Lord now, but it was not too late for her to learn to put Satan in his place.

Strategy 3: Doubt, unbelief and fear that God will not do for you what He has done, is doing and will do for others (Genesis 3). "He does not love you the same as He loves others. The doctor has more expertise than God. Are you sure God can do what He says?"

Strategy 4: *The battle for the mind* in which he plants some thought that is negative or destructive and tries to convince you that it is real and you cannot overcome it. Mark 5 finds a man who got consumed by something and it drove him crazy enough to make a graveyard his residence.

Strategy 5: *Attacking the Word of God*: He wants us to believe it doesn't work. It isn't real, true or exactly what He meant when He said it. It is open for interpretation.

Every person on the planet earth needs to be aware of these strategies so that Satan does not catch us by surprise. Knowledge of his tactics is critical in warfare. What good team does not study their opponent before facing them, especially in a run for the championship? You are a champion my friend. You must study the strategies of your opponent. You must be aware of where he has defeated you in the past, and where he is attacking in the present. It's not a game for him. He is in it for one season only. Its winner take all for him! It is a life or death match. He will tell you that you are okay with living a half way dedicated to God lifestyle. But half dedication is not dedicated. It is what Revelations calls "lukewarm". The Lord is never pleased with us half in and half out. If you are, you are a witness for the prosecution. He will accuse you when the time comes. He will convict your heart, so he can silence your tongue, just as you are preparing for your greatest testimony. Note the following scriptures and keep them close to your heart and tongue.

John 8:34 – "*[34]Jesus replied, "I tell you the truth, everyone who sins is a slave to sin."*

Ephesians 4:27 – "^{27}and do not give the devil a foothold."

Romans 1:18-27 – "^{18}The wrath of God is being revealed from heaven against all the godlessness and wickedness of men who suppress the truth by their wickedness, ^{19}since what may be known about God is plain to them, because God has made it plain to them. ^{20}For since the creation of the world God's invisible qualities—his eternal power and divine nature—have been clearly seen, being understood from what has been made, so that men are without excuse.

^{21}For although they knew God, they neither glorified him as God nor gave thanks to him, but their thinking became futile and their foolish hearts were darkened. ^{22}Although they claimed to be wise, they became fools ^{23}and exchanged the glory of the immortal God for images made to look like mortal man and birds and animals and reptiles.

^{24}Therefore God gave them over in the sinful desires of their hearts to sexual impurity for the degrading of their bodies with one another. ^{25}They exchanged the truth of God for a lie, and worshiped and served created things rather than the Creator—who is forever praised. Amen."

James 1:14-15, "^{14}but each one is tempted when, by his own evil desire, he is dragged away and enticed. ^{15}Then, after desire has conceived, it gives birth to sin; and sin, when it is full-grown, gives birth to death."

Ashamed

Awareness is not enough. The next intersection of intercession is *ashamed*. After you have begun to ask the Lord to reveal to you the strategies of Satan, and to show you every curse and or stronghold (via revelation or conversation with someone else who loves you), what you will have before you, is a pile of pain. If you are going to turn these ashes into beauty, then the first phase is to look upon it with shame. This is the intersection where *my* tears were uncontrollable. I cried in public. I cried in private. I cried in the shower, in the car. I cried at the steps of the pulpit (of the church God had called me to oversee)   Ashamed of the *me* that I had allowed myself to become, I wept bitterly. This shame was a direct result of studying and meditating on the life of Jesus. It is a purifying shame. It is a preparation for release from bondage shame. Often we make the mistake of comparing our lives to people and we generally come out pretty well, or at the very least adequate enough not to make any God honoring changes in our lives. Worship music was a key to my deliverance from personal demons, generational curses and strongholds. It drew me to the throne room, the very presence of God. There I saw my naked self. The shame of my nakedness, in addition to the scars I was personally accountable for placing on His body, I could not bear. To really discover, beyond the surface, how much God loves you, and then know how much you lived in ungratefulness, is painfully shameful. It was shame that drove me to fasting. I had to do something drastic. I was afraid of what I had become. I was afraid to share it with others. I hid it well. I drown my sorrow and suppressed my hidden wounds. I ran from problems. So, fasting was my only option. It was my last hope. Even doing it seemed to be fruitless in the beginning, because I didn't see it work immediately. Whatever you do in The Lord must be seen as a seed. Sometimes it takes a while to take root, but if you wait, you will see a wonderful harvest every time.

Whatever you do, press past the *ashamed* stage. The grief can be tough and people consider harming themselves here. Do **not** do it my friend! Every day with Jesus is better than the day before. Your pain has a purpose. LIVE to see it, and tell about it. Use your pain to set someone else free when you are ready. And, you *will* be ready. Your pain is a seed, for a harvest of deliverance for everyone who hears about it. You are the Lord's healing seed. Do not let that seed die before its time. Sow it, so it can see its harvest.

Agitated

My prayer time, like yours, had to come to this intersection. The cross road of agitation is the intersection where you become angry with sin in your life. *One*, you begin to see what it has stolen from your past. *Two*, you begin to see what you should have been, or should have accomplished, but couldn't or didn't. The years I spent in a bar consuming spirits, I should have been writing books, music, working on my marriage, raising a family and creating kingdom things! What a party the devil was having, watching wasted anointing spill into the streets of a city that needed every drop of it.

Have you ever counted, or attempted to add up all the money you wasted on sin? Thank God He *can* redeem the time. Every stage needs to be soaked in prayer, so you do not take a turn away from the pathway to perfection. Fasting and prayer keeps you from fits of rage, self-pity, hiding out and beating yourself up daily. Fasting and praying puts the fight in you to pursue the path you were born to pursue further. They keep agitation from turning into frustration. They help you to use it as a stairway to success. Failures are learning tools, not death notices. Now that I have made these discoveries, I am better equipped to achieve any task that surfaces. If I can overcome "*that*", I can overcome anything. Matthew 27:75 says that Peter wept, when he remembered the words Jesus had spoken to Him. He thought about what he was destined to be attached to, and saw his failure to stay focused. He arose slowly and positioned himself back in the ranks after trial and error.

Arrested

Acts 9 has the story of Saul's (Paul's) conversion. It is the intersection where you are arrested by the presence of God. I must share with you that it is much more pleasant to place yourself under arrest. Surrendering to Him willingly is less of a hassle. Fighting your arrest can cause damage to you. In Mark 9 the little boy, after Jesus arrested him, the spirit convulsed the boy he fell to the ground and foamed at the mouth. Arrest yourself, like the demon-possessed man in Mark 5, who saw Jesus and ran to him, falling down on his knees in front of Him. Give him permission to excuse every known and unknown spirit that has you.

When a person is under arrest, they surrender to the authority of another. Their will may not be broken, but their actions against the law are. They are then shackled, for security, so they cannot easily escape. So lift your hands and surrender. Lie prostrate before him in humble submission to Him. Your life is about to be transformed. Part two is to follow in the next chapter. Can you believe I spent so much time on this subject that I had to push it into two chapters? If I did, then it must be important. So let's get busy in our continued journey of breaking those strongholds and generational curses. Focus my friend. The best of your life is yet to come.

7
Canceling Generational Curses and Breaking Strongholds
Part II: The Bridge to the Future

> When you fast, you under nourish the soulish man but you build up the spirit man.
> Bishop Darryl. F. Husband

As we continue this journey it is necessary for you to know that there is an area of it that you will have to travel by yourself. It is the discovery time. It is the time of introspection. There is a time in every life that a person needs to be alone with themselves, so that they can seriously inspect their passions and motives. It is a time as well, where we completely open ourselves to the inspection of God. We become naked before Him. This is the bridge to your future. Press your way through this. There is a light at the end of the tunnel. The next area is *aloof.*

Aloof

To be aloof is to be distant or away from social relations. This is a key intersection, and is the bridge to your future. What you do at this intersection will determine much of what you will ultimately become in Christ. Acts 9 shows us the preparation stage for Paul's ministry. The bible shows us how in blindness, he has to go off alone to receive the mentoring of an unknown believer. This man with all of this intelligence has left behind him his old friends, but is not yet accepted by the new crowd of people, of which he has been led to be apart.

Listen my dear friend. This intersection is the one in which you come to and know that it's time to turn off your engine. It is the fueling station. It is the stage in which you tune up, get an oil change, and check the head lights, windshield wipers and all other fluids. I remember so well, this stage. It is a very lonely stage. God calls you away from the crowds. It is the offering of your "Isaac on the altar" stage. It is the, will you give your money to the poor, rich young ruler, stage. You are alone to make a decision about your life, and what direction you want to pursue. You cannot see your future, and your past is a blur. You are neither comfortable in your past, your future, nor your present. There are times in your life that God calls you to be alone with Him. He puts you in "image training".

Whenever you see what I call "image dementia" in your life, where you begin to forget who you are or whose you are, then it's time to be alone with Him. When you see worldly character traits taking root, it's time for "aloof" ministry. Fasting and praying calls you away from the world, to deal with *you*. There are some things you cannot break in a crowd, unless that crowd is strategically gathered for spiritual warfare and they are freedom fighters.

Mark 1:35 says, *"^{35}Very early in the morning, while it was still dark, Jesus got up, left the house and went off to a solitary place, where he prayed."* Jesus left the disciples early in the morning to go and pray. All of us need private prayer time. We need time away where we cannot hear any other voice, but the voice of the Father and experience the move of the Holy Spirit in our lives. There, at that crossroad, at that intersection of intercession, is where life change happens.

I will never forget that first season: rejection; cursed out; cancelled preaching engagements; recognition of true friendships; and fewer friends, but my needs were met. It was trying and test filled. Yet, it was the season that taught me to pray, to surrender to and believe God completely. It was the season that taught me how to say no to my flesh. It was the season that taught me to love myself, to repent, refocus and discern spirits as I go. It was the season that I began to see my assignment, to hear His voice, to know His love, to be *filled* with His Spirit, not just *talk* about it. It was the season the shackles of tradition were broken, and the beginning of becoming free to be the man of God I was created in His image to be, without having to be accepted by others.

The closer you come to Him, the more of the world you shed. The world impregnates us with many seeds that seek to attack us at many angles. Some of them have a greater pleasure level to our flesh than others. Before I came to Christ, I used profanity (only with the fellows). Afterwards, I never went back to it. The using of profanity never pleased me that much, so that was an easy release, but there were other seeds that were birthed, and grew up in me, that I married and became the parents of in other people. I taught them to drink, smoke, increase the passion for women, how to hide sin (even while in ministry). My "aloof" intersection happened while I was a pastor. As I write this book, I am mindful of the countless many that are still stuck in the mire of mediocrity. It is the lukewarm position in ministry that subjects itself to being the cause of sickness in the body of Christ. How could those who are leading be the source of sickness in the body? What a frightening portrait, sufficing to merely preach, yet never coming to the knowledge of the truth.

No, I did not get *caught* in sin, or a big public scandal. I was not sick, nor threatened death as some supposed. I arrested *myself,* and went on an "aloof ministry", because I wanted to please God. I wanted to experience His fullness. I tired of my flesh dominating my spirit man. I wanted to be a man of integrity. I wanted people to know God could change you if you let Him. I wanted them to know that ministers struggle and need deliverance too, and if any pastors, ministers of the five-fold ministry gifts needed a confidential counselor to coach them to their healthy place in Him, they could trust me.

Abortive

The abortive intersection is the intercession of casting off. The fasted life is designed to keep you casting off every weight that holds you back. In Matthew 4, Jesus practices the "aloof ministry" to prepare Himself for His assignment, and immediately the tempter comes and he casts off stuff as it was thrown on Him. He didn't let anything stick. Fasting and prayer prepares you to cast off, abort any evil seed before they take root, or to abort them afterwards if need be.

Four things I needed in this stage to help me and that will also help you through: angels, a heavenly prayer language, an unrelenting passion for the heart of God, and a love for yourself and others you affect daily. Note the following scriptures:

1. Hebrews 1:14; 2:1 – *"[14]Are not all angels ministering spirits sent to serve those who will inherit salvation? [1]We must pay more careful attention, therefore, to what we have heard, so that we do not drift away."*

2. Romans 8:26-28 – *"[26]In the same way, the Spirit helps us in our weakness. We do not know what we ought to pray for, but the Spirit himself intercedes for us with groans that words cannot express. [27]And he who searches our hearts knows the mind of the Spirit, because the Spirit intercedes for the saints in accordance with God's will. [28]And we know that in all things God works for the good*

of those who love him who have been called according to his purpose."

    3. Jude 1:20 – *"[20]But you, dear friends, build yourselves up in your most holy faith and pray in the Holy Spirit."*
    4. I Corinthians 13:1 – *"[1]If I speak in the tongues of men and of angels, but have not love, I am only a resounding gong or a clanging cymbal."*

    Angels, prayer language and love of God, self and others, will assist you in aborting your old life and mission. Search the scripture to discover that angels are waiting to war in your behalf. Ask God for the gift of the Holy Spirit with the evidence of speaking in tongues. You will (like I did), discover that it is not for Pentecostals alone, but for Christians. It is not "denominational", it is demon "destruction-al". I prayed without understanding, about issues I may have never prayed about on my own, until strongholds were broken, and generational curses were revealed and cancelled. Glory to God!

    Finally, there is no substitute for love. Matthew 22:37 – 40 – *"[37]Jesus replied: "'Love the Lord your God with all your heart and with all your soul and with all your mind.' [38]This is the first and greatest commandment. [39]And the second is like it: 'Love your neighbor as yourself.' [40]All the Law and the Prophets hang on these two commandments."* If you do not love God, you will never truly inspect yourself to the point to find out what pleases Him and then seek to change any quality about yourself that conflicts with that. As you do that reflective surgery, you begin to see how your *"dis-eased"* self, has affected countless others inside and outside of the body of Christ. If you love them, you will seek to correct the wrong, and exemplify a new standard. Self inflicted wounds can be healed, and with the right guidance those people make excellent physicians. Love is a key ingredient in the process.

Alive

Congratulations, you are either a new born or you are reborn, as Peter was, in Luke 22:31. Jesus told him, "After you are strengthened, strengthen the brethren." This intersection is the freedom stage. This is the dancing stage. It is the second weeping stage. This time, it is pure joy. There comes a time in your fasting and praying, that you are as pure as "truth". Your vision is clear. Your inordinate passions are in your past, and are no longer threatening to suffocate your witness. The prescription called fasting is in your system. You are getting used to living on heaven's bread, and taking in the earth's, as there is a need not a craving.

This is the stage where you learn to walk and talk again as well. It is important at this stage to get someone who has driven where you are going, to ride with you, like Ananias did with Saul. You just had your eyes dilated, been in vision screening. You have just been tested for new optical wear. You *will* see differently now. Do not be ashamed, even if you are a seasoned pastor, to get someone to help you walk out this dimension. The future is too exciting for setbacks.

Appreciative

While there are times during the "alive" stage, that you feel growing pains as any child does, the past is too painful to return to. Israel must have been crazy. When you get a true revelation of who God is, and then one of who you are, you will begin a praise and worship celebration that will never cease. I sometimes stop to ask myself, what was I thinking? How could I have allowed people to get me to believe, that any other way but holiness was the most satisfying way to live? I have been on both sides in the church. It is not even close.

Here is the stage where you investigate the following names of God. Take the time to tell God often (as I did and do), how much you appreciate Him. Daily I let Him know that I am so appreciative of His grace in my life. It is an honor to be a part of His family. It is awesome to know as well that what is in Him is also in me. Let's take a look and see what our Fathers personality is and what ours should have in it as well. Stop at each of these and thank Him for being each one of these areas in your life. Then ask Him to make you that example in someone else's life.

    El-Gibhor – Mighty God
    Jehovah Jireh – The Lord who provides
    Jehovah M'kaddesh – The Lord who sanctifies
    Jehovah Tsidkenu – The Lord our righteousness
    Jehovah Rapha – The Lord our healer
    Jehovah Shalom – The Lord is peace
    Jehovah Sabbaoth – The Lord of Hosts
    Elohim – God (mighty, strong and powerful)
    El Shaddai – God Almighty
    El Roi – The Strong One who sees
    Jehovah Rohi – The Lord is my Shepherd

Now we are ready to move the next intersection of intercession. It is called the intersection of "aggressive". A change is taking place before your very eyes and your engine is revving up ready to go.

Aggressive

I heard Dr. Charles Stanley, preaching about the Apostle Paul, make reference to the fact that when Jesus interrupted his journey and changed his life that he never got over it. He spent the rest of his life in passionate pursuit of closeness with Christ. Philippians 3:10 is a snapshot of that passion. He says, "That I might know Him, in the power of His resurrection". When you hear Paul talk, it is as if he only has a day or two left to live and he wants to get it all in. Listen further as he says, "putting those things behind me, I press towards the mark of the high calling which is in Christ Jesus" (Verse 14). When you are fasting and there is an area of concern in your life, make sure you aggressively tackle that area. If you have had issues in an area, put enough Word on it, that it never lifts its ugly head again. Cancel its desire in your flesh once and for all. Cut it to the core. Build a list of scriptures that you can refer to at will, in case you sense for any reason, that Satan is trying to reintroduce that desire to you. Meet him head on, with the only thing he respects. He will respect the strength of your "It is written". You must have that sword readily available if you have had a family history or a personal long standing addiction. As a matter of fact, do not wait for him to come, make confessions of your faith in every season where you used to turn to sin, until he sees his offering to you of your past, as a fruitless venture.

Second Corinthians 10:5 says this, *"⁵We demolish arguments and every pretension that sets itself up against the knowledge of God, and we take captive every thought to make it obedient to Christ."* The nature of our weapons is found in Ephesians 6:13-18,

> *"¹³Therefore put on the full armor of God, so that when the day of evil comes, you may be able to stand your ground, and after you have done everything, to stand. ¹⁴Stand firm then, with the belt of truth buckled around your waist, with the breastplate of righteousness in place, ¹⁵and with your feet fitted with the readiness that comes from the gospel of peace. ¹⁶In addition to all this, take up the shield of faith, with which you can extinguish all the flaming arrows of the evil one. ¹⁷Take the helmet of salvation and the sword of the Spirit, which is the word of God. ¹⁸And pray in the Spirit on all occasions with all kinds of prayers and requests. With this in mind, be alert and always keep on praying for all the saints."*

As you can see, we *are* in a fight, but one that is fixed. We win! However, we must use our weapons daily as a reminder to the enemy that we will not to be caught off guard. There will be *NO* entrance into the body on my watch. Say it again, this time with boldness. ***There Will Be NO Entrance to the Body of Christ on My Watch***! I will keep my armor on at all times and watch as well as pray so that the enemy sees futility of effort when it comes to opposing me. Take a look at your armor and begin to put it on.

Truth – Being honest (in love Ephesians 4:15) with yourself and others always.

Righteousness – Living holy, beyond reproach

Walking out the Gospel of Peace – Being at peace with others, sharing the gospel

Faith – Trusting God for everything and with everything. He owns it all, even me!

Protecting the Mind – Know you're saved! Romans 10:9-10 – *"^{9}That if you confess with your mouth, "Jesus is Lord," and believe in your heart that God raised him from the dead, you will be saved. ^{10}For it is with your heart that you believe and are justified, and it is with your mouth that you confess and are saved."* Hebrews 11:1, {MSG} – *"^{1}The fundamental fact of existence is that this trust in God, this faith, is the firm foundation under everything that makes life worth living. It's our handle on what we can't see."* Hebrews 11:6 {MSG} – *"^{6}It's impossible to please God apart from faith. And why? Because anyone who wants to approach God must believe both that he exists and that he cares enough to respond to those who seek him."*

The Sword of the Spirit – We have spent quite a bit of time dealing with the power and authority of the Word of God.
Derek Prince, in Lucifer Exposed, offers what he calls the "seventh weapon", in which I mentioned earlier. He calls our attention to Ephesians 6:18 {KJV} which is beyond the

armor, and at the end of that chapter. Here is what it says, *"¹⁸Praying always with all prayer and supplication in the Spirit, and watching thereunto with all perseverance and supplication for all saints."* He says, "Prayer is our means of breaking out of the restrictions of reaching only as far as our arm will extend. Prayer is limitless. It is our "intercontinental ballistic missile." We can launch it from anywhere and make it land anywhere. In the weapon of prayer, there are three main components to do the job: the Word of God (the *logos*); the name of Jesus; and the blood of Jesus.[17] I want to reiterate, that this weapon is priceless. It saved my life. We move now to the eleventh intersection. It is the one in which you begin to see your worth restored and your power to practice what is in you surfacing. It is a stage of caution. Do not move too quickly until you know all you have and are able to operate in it without causing damage. It is the "anointed" intersection.

Anointed

The eleventh intersection of intercession is the preparation stage for your purpose. Here you recognize that God has gifted you. You should take a spiritual gift's assessment, if you have never done one. You should make sure you are connected to the right place in the body. Not only should you check *where* you are serving (the church), but the *ministry* you do in that church. You are gifted to serve somewhere. You are equipped to heal the sick, reach the lost, disciple them into the faith, and prepare them to do the same. You are not just born anew to sit, but to serve. You have in you the yoke destroying, burden removing power of God that has freed you, and will free others to reach their God designed destiny. Your voice has been *restored*, as an authority in the atmosphere. When you speak, things happen. You are positioned in "sonship". The *earth* respects you, and is waiting for you to command it. You are anointed to cast out demons.

---

[17] Derek Prince, *Lucifer Exposed*, Whitaker House, New Kensington, PA, 2006, pg 63

The power of God, the authority of Christ lives in you. You have arrived at the status of Ambassador in the earth. Accept your position and walk in your authority. Learn everything you can about who you are now, so that you can fulfill your calling. You are a Kingdom Ambassador assigned to the earth to prepare people for the Kings arrival. You are on the preparation team to establish the kingdom order in the land. Wherever you reside, work and worship is your jurisdiction. Let s move further as we go to the final intersection of intercession, "assignment".

Assignment

The twelfth and final intersection of intercession is the place where you spend the rest of your life. You see your purpose for being there, and you pursue it with passion. You know who you have been assigned to, and where you have been assigned, and you may experience some burdens with the assignment, but you have grace to help you through every moment. You soon will discover that nothing gives you more joy. Suddenly, ministry is neither a bore nor drudgery. You actually get to the place where you cannot wait to serve. You now look for opportunities, to do what I am doing with you in this book. You ask yourself, "How can I use this joy to help others find their way?"

I close this chapter with a testimony from one of my brothers in the faith, Bishop Larry Jackson. He tells the story of his young life in his book, Guilt Free Living, which led to his assignment to men in the body of Christ.

> *"When I was 10 years old, my next-door neighbor took advantage of me sexually. He was a relative of my best friend. Both of us thought he was cool. Since we were best friends, I was a regular visitor at his house as he was mine. One Saturday afternoon, I went to his house and discovered that my friend and his mother had gone shopping. We were the only ones in the*

house at the time when he asked me to help him with something. Much of what took place leading up to this man getting on top of me remains a blur, but God protected me in that there was no intercourse. He only laid on top of me and rubbed his body against mine, as I wondered how to get out of the room. To this day, I can remember the smell of his breath for he was a chain smoker. I was too afraid to tell anyone about what had happened, but I decided that I would never be alone with this man again. I also knew if my family found out about this, they would hurt this man. Consequently, I kept all of it inside. In order to prove to myself and to everyone else who may have thought I was gay, the way this man probably thought, I pursued women vigorously. Like so many abuse victims, I became very promiscuous. This violation opened the door to lust and, before I knew it, I was under its full control. After a while, sex and sexual activity became a major preoccupation. At first, this was a very desirable way to live but soon it became a secret nightmare. Many of my male friends told me how they wished they could live the life I was leading. They just did not understand how much pain I was in at the end of an evening of "fun". Even after I became a Christian, this way of life sought every opportunity to take advantage of any unsuspecting female who thought I was a nice guy. Because of the type of church I attended at the time, it was okay to date; so I did. I wanted Jesus but could not find true and lasting freedom from this evil desire. Each time I thought it was over and I had broken lust's hold, without warning, I would find myself back in a similar situation. I would cry out to God and start over with even greater determination. And so the cycle continued. After 12 long years of struggling, I finally reached the point where I was no longer willing to tolerate the control Satan had over me. I was determined to be free! After coming to a place where everything I my life was falling apart, I had to return to my father's home to live. My father was a Church of God in Christ pastor in a small city outside of Petersburg, Virginia. He had all of the Christian books and materials I would ever need. The more I learned from these books and the new church I attended, under the leadership of Bishop Wellington Boone, the more I wanted to be free of all lust. One Wednesday afternoon around 4 o'clock, the desire for freedom came to my heart so strongly that I immediately went to my bedroom, closed the door, fell to my knees and cried out to God for help. I was so desperate that I vowed not to leave until I was completely free. Not only did I walk out of that room completely free, but God also gave me an understanding that would prove to be extremely valuable in helping other people get free as well. From that day until this, whenever the opportunity presents itself, I share with people how they can experience the same freedom I experienced on that fateful day. As a result, I have seen God miraculously work in the lives of people who believed they could never experience true freedom from this powerful force." [18]

---

[18] Bishop Larry Jackson, *Guilt Free Living*- Frontliners Men's Ministries, Charlotte, NC, 2003, pg 5-7

What is your assignment my friend? There are people waiting for your story to be the seed for their deliverance. Through the fasted life, you can conquer every stronghold, and break forever, every generational curse in your family. Your family name will be covered by the blood of Jesus throughout eternity just like mine was and is. When you take your exit from this world into the next, what is the legacy you have been assigned to leave? Are you fulfilling it now? What are you waiting for? Do you need a push? Get to someone's office, or get to a seminar and get some training in the areas of your giftedness. You only have a short window of opportunity. The Kingdom of God is waiting for your role to be played, and people are waiting for your life to be sown. I am excited for you. I see you in the future and it is a glorious thing watching you receive your crowns of achievements. Hallelujah!

8
Fasting: The Key to Revelation for the Vision Impaired

> *"Through fasting . . .I have found a perfect health, a new state of existence, a feeling of purity and happiness, something unknown to humans."--Upton Sinclair (1878-1968, American writer)*

When I mention that this chapter is for the vision impaired, I do not mean in the natural. That would mean I would have written the book or at least this chapter in larger print or in Braille. While I would without question recommend fasting to those with a physical impairment as well, I was actually referring to people in the body of Christ, the local church, who find it difficult to see the vision of their house (church), communicated through their man or woman of God. It is also for those who cannot see their personal worth or vision nor the vision for their family. I have been, in recent years, struck by the words in John 3:3 which say, *"[3]In reply Jesus declared, "I tell you the truth, no one can see the kingdom of God unless he is born again."* Unless a man is born again, he cannot <u>see</u> the Kingdom of God. There are some things you cannot see or understand outside of being born again, dead to another life. Fasting is the way to keep your old life dead, destroyed, distraction free, so you can see, understand, focus on the assignment God has for you as a new person in Christ.

Coming to know Jesus as our personal savior is a one-time deal. We accept the fact that He died for our sins and His blood cleansed our sins, making us now the righteousness of God in Christ Jesus. On the other hand, it is a life time of work to make Him Lord of our lives. We must work diligently to keep Him on the throne room of our heart. We must daily crucify our flesh, keeping it so that it does not rise up and take charge again. Fasting on a regular basis is the answer to this, "keeping Jesus as Lord".

When we have to struggle with our personal lives: integrity; attitude; keeping our marriage intact; walking in love; living holy; etc. we often do not have energy to serve, to win souls or to advance the kingdom. The old adage is true, you cannot build a city fighting a war.

Bob Wall, Robert Solum and Mark Sobol wrote the book, The Visionary Leader. It is a book that all pastors and their leadership teams should read. They begin chapter 2, "The Leaders New Role", by saying *"No plan or vision, regardless of the cleverness or quality of its design, will work without enlightened leadership to carry it out."* They go on to say, *"The new leader has two primary roles. One is to have a vision and implement it. The other is to prepare people in the company to assume greater responsibility."* They found that often, leaders had not developed strong vision for their corporations, and that the problem came because they had not been willing to let go of what they called, "the mules". The concept came from a story of an old Army sergeant who had been serving out his career early in the 20th century. He was a life-long "mule skinner", caring for the animals that pulled the cannons for the Army. Just as he was getting ready to retire, the Army started to use motor vehicles to pull their cannons instead of the mules. Strangely though, the old sergeant continued to stand behind the cannons with his arms out stretched. Someone asked what he was doing and the reply came back that he was still holding on to the mules. The authors added this observation,

> *"Though some managers may not be able to let go of old habits, for others the unwillingness to change goes even deeper. These managers in the long run, will be the biggest obstacles to the new leader's vision. They are going to resist change at all costs either because it doesn't occur to them that they need to change or they believe the false notion that the change will force them to relinquish their personal power. The old structure has provided them with a direct span of control that they are comfortable with. Giving up that power is difficult, especially for those who lack an understanding of the new vision... Out of fear, they are blowing the opportunity of a lifetime to grasp perhaps the most satisfying and profitable power of all: the chance to help others empower themselves."[19]*

Many churches fail to have significant progress because of this sad reality. Likewise, many individuals stall their lives, or live far beneath their potential, because they lack vision or hang on to philosophies and failures of people they respect. The holding on to of the "traditions of men", have stagnated the personal and corporate growth of the church.

Ephesians 1:17-19 {NKJV} is a prayer that every Christian needs to focus their attention on early in their walk,

> *"[17]that the God of our Lord Jesus Christ, the Father of glory, may give to you the spirit of wisdom and revelation in the knowledge of Him, [18]the eyes of your understanding being enlightened; that you may know what is the*

---

[19] Bob Wall, Robert S. Solum, Mark R. Sobol, *The Visionary Leader*, Prima Publishing, Rocklin, CA, 1992, pg 21

> *hope of His calling, what are the riches of the glory of His inheritance in the saints, [19]and what is the exceeding greatness of His power toward us who believe, according to the working of His mighty power"*

The problem with too many Christians is three-fold: blindness; far-sightedness; or, rearview-sightedness. The children of Israel are an example of all three. Initially they could not see. Their enslavement numbed their ability to focus beyond their circumstances. They accepted their condition as permanent and lost sight of their created worth. Then, they only had the ability to see the wilderness after they were freed from their past. Tragically they walked in utter darkness without faith. They had a promise that was told to be in front of them, but their vision was obscured by fear, anger, and rebellion.

Hearing is a great gift from God, but seeing it after you hear it, is invaluable. To be free and yet suffer the inability to see where you are going is sad and dangerous. Freedom always needs a plan attached to it. It always needs a map to go along side of it. You are not really free because you are released from your past, if you have no plan to pursue a purpose in your future. Wanderers are merely experiencing an alternate bondage. It is called the bondage of indecisiveness. It is a holding pattern. My future appears to be bright because I am no longer held by what I knew was life threatening. I am so excited about being free from that past that I fail to realize that I am in as dangerous a position as ever because I do not know where I am going and therefore am in position for greatness or the grave, whichever possesses me first.

My potential may be powerful, but it has no drawing power, nothing at which to aim, so it can never be realized. As time passes, frustration seeps in and instigates a return to familiar ground. There you will find comfort (not peace). It is seldom dark in our past. We can always find a false illumination back to bondage. The darkness always lies in the unseen future where it takes faith to walk into. The light we need to get there is unfamiliar and blinding. It often comes by way of people who push us beyond our comfort. They see more in us than we see in ourselves. Rebellion is often the result. Moses is a prime example. He saw what God saw for the children of Israel. They saw Egypt and wilderness, he saw Canaan, the Promised Land. Conflict ensued, and the ones that could not see what their leader saw, died without experiencing true freedom. Revelation is the key to freedom.

If indeed revelation is the key to freedom, then it is certain that every person on the planet needs it. If you intend to get free from something that has you bound, then you need revelation on how to escape. If you are free from bondages, then you need revelation on how to stay free. You need help seeing every trap set for you, and knowing how to avoid them.

Fasting turns a light on inside of you. It refuses the voices of darkness to speak when it's time for instruction or direction. It illuminates the food you put inside you and draws its strength and sight from that food. Since the Word of God is your primary food during a fast, your strength and sight are drawn from it. Psalm 119:105 says, *"[105] Your word is a lamp to my feet and a light for my path."*

Do not let the storms of sandy deserts decide your destiny. No dry season is permanent unless you choose to fast *from* the Word of God. Every darkness you face, is a conquerable foe, when you are holding the weapon called the "Sword of the Spirit", which is the Word of God. Every famine you face is "overcome able" with a Word from God. It is His word that reveals escape routes in the midst of seemingly overwhelming circumstances. Famines may cause death in the world, but they are not meant for the death of God's children. Death for us is merely a transition anyway. We are not permanent death dwellers. We were born again to live eternally. Therefore, for us, famines call for three (3) things: discipline; discernment and defining. Allow me to explain.

Discipline

Discipline is defined as *"control gained by enforcing obedience or order"*[20] Whenever you are faced with famines, lack, challenges or painful circumstances in your life, it is critical that you are able to persevere. Well, now you have a choice. You either persevere, or perish. Okay, so you choose to persevere. I thought you would. If you had not, I would have taken the rest of this book to help you change your mind (as a matter of fact I have, because you need a **long** fast). As I am writing this book, the United States of America is facing economic times such as has not been seen since the "great depression" of the early 1930's. I would say this is close to, if not compared to, a season of famine. Discipline is crucial, because you have to learn to do everything in moderation in seasons like this. You learn to eat less. You practice spending less. You change habits that have been acquired simply because you had excess. You assess your needs, and then live life based on them, while saying to your wants, "Okay, I will feed you if and when I can". Even if I am privileged to have more than most in a famine, it is not flaunting season. It becomes a season that I learn how I can use some of my wealth to serve others. I make my wants wait or I sacrifice them permanently. It may be that they surface again in another season, but I may decide I am better off without them.

Fasting is a great famine fighter in more than one way. First, if you learn to fast before a famine approaches, you are already disciplined to do without certain things. Therefore, excluding them or separating yourself from them is not a major surgery decision. Secondly, if you fast during a famine, because it is a life-style, not a forced economic move, then your flesh will know, that it is submitting in expectation of enlightenment, which will benefit its future. You see, the flesh even benefits by getting to hang around longer. It is "dead" in

---

[20] *Merriam-Webster Online Dictionary* Merriam-Webster, Incorporated, 2005

the sense that it does not rule, totally submitted to the Spirit of the Lord within you, but it is glowing because it is the outer representation of the spirit. The flesh is cleansed on a fast. As it is healed, it becomes younger, and a stronger servant after a fast.

Have you ever considered that you need to be able to see the future when a famine is present? Blindness is a death warrant waiting to happen. Joseph saw seven (7) strong years and then seven (7) lean years while he was interpreting a vision. Genesis 41:29-30, *"^{29} Seven years of great abundance are coming throughout the land of Egypt, ^{30} but seven years of famine will follow them. Then all the abundance in Egypt will be forgotten, and the famine will ravage the land."* He saw the famine before it came, so he set up a plan to make it through. You can have that kind of revelation too. If you will draw near to God, He will show you what He sees. The closer you are to Him, the better your revelation. Fasting eliminates the wasteful world in your life and allows you to experience the wonder of the God-kind of life. You see life the way He sees it. What a joy!

Discernment

To discern means *"to come to know or recognize mentally."*[21] What are the signs of the times? That is what Joseph was gifted to know. Can you see what every season requires you to see as it approaches? Or, do you see better while you are in it? Obviously, the better of the two is to see before it approaches. II Kings 6 has a great account of a "seer". I love this story. Elisha could *see* the enemy attacking at a certain venue (before it the day arrived), and so he told the king of Israel and they were able to prepare for the battle in advance, not just deal with it as it was happening. It was said about Elisha that he could hear in the enemies' bedroom, in the

---

[21] *Merriam-Webster Online Dictionary* Merriam-Webster, Incorporated, 2005

enemy's battle strategy war room. Hell cannot hide its plans to harm you, your family, ministry, business, community, city or anything connected to you. It has a plan of attack. The question is, can you hear and see it in advance, or do you have to wait until it happens and endure unnecessary casualties en route to your victory? You *will* win, but *how*, is the question.

Can you see why your ability to see is so significant? Well, let's keep building your faith to this end, so you never cease to believe it. I Chronicles 12:32 {NASB} says, *"³²Of the sons of Issachar, men who understood the times, with knowledge of what Israel should do..."* Now take out Sons of Issachar and Israel. _____ understood the times and knew what _____ should do. Do you see your name in the first blank and your family in the second? Do you see your name in the first blank and your ministry in the second, or your church, community, business? Glen Martin and Gary McIntosh write in their book, The Issachar Factor; *"The Bible says that where there is not vision, the people perish. Our vision shapes us. Our vision controls us. Our vision determines who and what we become. Our vision of how we want to look determines the clothing we buy, the hairstyle we have and the accessories we wear. Our vision of what a family is determines what our family life is like. Our vision of what a marriage is determines what our marriage becomes. Likewise, vision shapes our leadership."*

In the first chapter of Martin and McIntosh's book, they offer us a compelling, convincing argument for why knowing the times, discernment, is so important. They compare the ages we have lived in: Agricultural – 1860; Industrial 1860-1956; and Information 1956-Present. Cities, companies, churches and individuals who have not changed with the ages, have died. [22] My mother in law noted that she was once a salesperson. She sold wigs (hair extensions or replacements). She commented in laughter, about their unpopularity at the time she was selling

---

[22] Glen Martin and Gary McIntosh, *The Issachar Factor*, Broadman & Holman Publishers, Nashville, TN, 1993, pg 57-58

them. I told her she sold them in the wrong era. In some cultures she could do very, very well selling wigs and hair pieces today. Timing is everything. If you cannot *see*, or have revelation, you could suffer loss, or possibly not experience prosperity because of it.

Defining

By this, I mean, ones character is discovered. You may not be able to see a person's true character in good times, but it is shaped and defined in famine seasons. It is in trying times that we learn most about ourselves. We learn about ourselves what we need to work on most. Famines define who and what you are devoted to, the world, or God. You discover what you can be bought for. By this I mean, the answer will come to, what amount you will sell out your values for. It *will* be seen in a famine season. In Genesis, there are two accounts in the life of Abraham, when he was in, what I call, "father of our faith school", where he handed his wife over and lied about his relationship, so he could save his own life. He didn't fully trust God yet. He could not have died. He did not have any children yet. The promise had not yet been fulfilled. Yet, Abraham had not fully obtained his ability to see what God was saying to him. He did not have a clear revelation of who he was, nor who had told him his future. He *heard* the future. He initially acted in obedience, but challenges defined him, instead of the word that God gave him. Fasting is the key to seeing yourself as God sees you. You *do* become what you eat. Your vision, revelation of yourself, who you are and who you will become, is defined by your eating habits. Scheduling your meals and what is in them (spiritually), will determine supernatural sight, or merely natural sight, which is blindness into the unseen world in which you have an account, where you can draw from at will (or faith). Yet, if you cannot see it, you do not know it is there for you to draw from it.

Fasting is the character defining element that every one of us needs. It helps allow us to sing the words of a song I wrote, "I can see better now, I can hear clearly now…"

Rick Joyner writes, *"After observing Jesus' magnificent transfiguration, "Peter answered!" No one was even addressing Peter! And what came out of his mouth? "It is good for us to be here…I WILL." Sound familiar? True, it was good for them to be there…but not for Peter's reasons. It was good for them to glimpse the glory of their Lord. It was good for them to heed the Father's rebuke: "Hear Him." They were not there to hear Moses (a type of the Law), or Elijah (a type of the Church) but to hear Jesus! After they heard the command it is recorded: "Lifting up their eyes, they saw no one, except Jesus Himself alone." This was the purpose for which they had been brought to the mountain — their vision was to be focused on Him alone."*[23]

Is that not what you signed up for? Is that not what you desire to do? Do you not want to see Him? Don't you want to hear Him more clearly? You want to get to the place where every other voice is secondary. The ideal place for us is the place where every other vision is secondary. Peter missed it. The object of our being with Him is not to build monuments to mortal men, but to see that He stands alone as God. His way is the only way.

When John 3:3 says, unless a man is born again, he cannot see the kingdom of God (which we will further discuss in chapter 8), he reveals to us the key to the God-kind of life, life more abundant. He clearly indicates that the key to vision is death to your own understanding of the way life should be viewed. You now ascribe to a biblical world view. You have a born again life. To be "Born again" means to have a second

---

[23] Joyner, Rick, *There Were Two Trees in the Garden*, Charlotte, NC, Morning Star Publications, 1984, pg 60-61

birth. It means death to the old life as we have referred to in a prior chapter.

Many people have joined churches, but never joined the body of Christ. You cannot *join* the Body of Christ. You have to die to be born into it. By death as we have already explained, we me to put aside living life by your feelings, emotions, and way of thinking. This is the way to new eyesight, revelation. You now see yourself as a part of a "royal priesthood, a holy nation, a chosen generation (II Peter 2:9). You become an ambassador for your King. You willingly serve in love, adding to your faith every necessary thing to equip you with what you need to fulfill your King's assignment. When people come into the church and do not see this, often, they operate in di-vision, mis-representation and ir-revelation. Accidents and casualties are the result of their way of behavior. It is not without repentance however. They can reverse the pattern. Fasting is the answer. Thank God through Jesus, every pathway of death, while we are in the earth, is the pathway to resurrection and revelation. It is time to SEE my friend. No matter what death you have experienced or if your name has had casualty written all over it. Today is "revelation for a resurrection", day. Glory to God!

9
Fasting As a Sabbath-
Your Body Needs Rest-oration

> *Fating is not an end in itself; it is a means by which we can worship the Lord and submit ourselves in humility to Him. We don't make God love us any more than He already does if we fast, or if we fast longer. Fasting invites God into the problem. Then in the strength of God, victory is possible. - Elmer L. Towns*

I sincerely believe that fasting extended my life. There are foods I no longer eat, nor beverages I no longer drink. This change came as a result of fasting. It was fasting (and prayer/worship), that broke a night-time drinking and smoking ritual. It was fasting that got me into bed at an earlier hour so that I could rest more. It was fasting that has extended my life. Oh, did I say that already? Well, it was worth repeating.

Genesis 1 says that God created the earth's atmospheric use in six days and on the seventh day he "sabbathed". He rested. Why did God need a rest? Was He tired? Does He get tired of speaking? Well, maybe to us when we are ignoring His counsel, but otherwise, no. So why the Sabbath? Why does

God say, "He rested?" I believe that it means God reflected. God took time after a season of work to reflect on what He had done to make certain that it met His standards. Excellence or perfection is His way. Good is a part of His holy character. After His work He reflected to see that which He said was matching His character and way. Obviously, what He said was the same as what He did. That goes without saying when speaking of Him. It should also be the trademark, character trait, of His children. So far, at least one of them got it right (Jesus).

Notice this, man was created after reflecting. His greatest creation was made after reflection, a pause. His breath then breathed out an image of the creator Himself. It is easier to reproduce His image after proper time to reflect, pause, breathe and rest. Many people never produce, create good, above average, the supernatural consistent with their creative worth, because they never stop to reflect, pause, breathe and rest. In this chapter we will explore fasting as a Sabbath, a reflection, rest, a time to allow your total self to breathe. You need it whether you know it now or not, so come on, let's get to it.

My wife almost has to make me take vacations, because I can get consumed in work. Sometimes she and my administrator have blocked off a week's time on my calendar, and will refuse to allow anyone to interfere with that time. They do that because they think that if it were up to me, I would never stop. Come on, what do they think I think I am, a machine (smile)? Time and time again I have noticed that whenever we go away, I spend the first day in the bed sleeping. That is strange because I would not do that at home. I wear shorts and sandals and cannot seem to get enough of one thing, rest. It is simply amazing. Then, just about the time to return, I experience a download of ideas and we are talking ministry without pressure to work, but a natural flow into who we are and what we do.

The body and the mind need rest. The mind is in the constant mode of delivery, eating, drinking, thinking, receiving a plethora of information, mostly damaging or destructive which needs processing. That is our life. We live in a highly technological, fast paced world. Not to rest is to retire early (to the grave).

Dr. Don Colbert, (a unique medical doctor), in his book Toxic Relief, said this,

> *"Fasting allows your body to heal by giving it a rest. All living things need to rest, including you. Even the land must rest, which was a principle God gave to the ancient agrarian Jewish nation regarding their fields. Every seventh year they were not permitted to grow any crops at all. They had to let the land lie fallow so that it could reestablish its own mineral and nutrient content (See Leviticus 25:1-7). Today, we live in a time in which farmers have completely forgotten this age-old principle. This is one of the factors involved in our being overfed and undernourished. It's because much of our soil is depleted that our food sources have also become partially depleted of the minerals, vitamins and other nutrients that our bodies crave. When we eat and don't get the nutrition we need from our food, we will usually eat more, trying to fill the body's craving for nourishment. Before long, we have become obese, overfed and undernourished. Every winter many animals will hibernate or rest for a season. Every night when you sleep, you give rest to your body and mind. Blessed rest is as much a law of the universe as gravity. It's also a powerful principle of healing. Think about it: When an animal is injured or sick, what does it do? It*

finds a resting place where it can lap up water, and it quits eating while it heals. This is natural, instinctual wisdom that God placed within the animal kingdom. But when our bodies get sick, what do we do? When we get sick with an injury or illness, such as pneumonia, a sinus infection or strep throat, instead of resting and fasting by drinking water or juices only, we eat ice cream, puddings, creamy soups and other rich, high-calorie foods that do nothing to cleanse and detoxify the body." [24]

He is crying out in a noise filled world, "Stop, listen, rest, be restored." Yet the noise and the mirages of pleasure entice us to send our bodies to premature cancellation of life. What could we do if we could hear the wise counsel of such physicians? What more would we accomplish? What if we really allowed ourselves to be influenced by the Bible? I heard one of the speakers of a convention I attended long ago say this, "It is not how much you go through the bible that really matters. It is how much the bible goes through you." It was a quaint little phrase I used in my preaching for many years. It always aroused a cheer or hearty Amen in people. However, it was years before I internalized it and saw it not just as a tool for preaching, but for living. In other words, it was not just a tool for others to be stroking my ego with how many phrases I could use to make people respond with shouts. It actually was food for me to live on. Thank God I matured past that stage. What was I thinking? God forgive me! Thank God for the blood of Jesus.

Wayne Muller says in his book Sabbath:

"We, too, must have a period in which we lie fallow, and restore our souls. In Sabbath time we remember to celebrate what is beautiful and sacred; we light candles, sing songs, tell

---

[24] Don Colbert, MD, *Toxic Relief*, Siloam, Lake Mary, FL, 2001, pg 46-47.

stories, eat, nap, and make love. It is a time to let our work, our lands, our animals lie fallow, to be nourished and refreshed. Within this sanctuary, we become available to the insights and blessings of deep mindfulness that arise only in stillness and time. When we act from a place of deep rest, we are more capable of cultivating what the Buddhists would call right understanding, right action, and right effort. In a complex and unstable world, if we do not rest, if we do not surrender into some kind of Sabbath, how can we find our way, how can we hear the voices that tell us the right thing to do?" [25]

Ever notice that football players, at some positions, often end their careers with nagging, lasting injuries and die at earlier ages than other athletes? Well, they spend every day in a car crash, an accident, where their bodies are willingly thrown, beaten and bruised. They use their heads, where their body receives its messages to function or not, as a weapon to fight with. Imagine being in a car accident every day. What trauma would that cause the body? The brain? After games, the following day is generally a day off. A day of rest. The body needs to recuperate from its crashes.

In weight lifting, a trainer will tell you to work on different body parts on different days. They will tell you not to do the same body part every day. For instance if you work on legs today, take tomorrow to work on arms. Why? You tear the muscle one day. Then you give it a day to rest, repair and build or grow. You are also told after a workout to eat, but eat right. Do not eat fatty or unhealthy foods. The key is to feed your damaged, torn, dead-like muscles, food that will help them grow to make you stronger. That is why fasting is about, "a *Sabbath* for your strength".

---

[25] Wayne Muller, *Sabbath*, Bantham Books, New York, NY, 1999, pg 7.

Exodus 20:8 says, *"⁸ "Remember the Sabbath day by keeping it holy."* I believe the Sabbath was written as a protection for human kind. If you do not have sense enough to stop on your own, then let's make it a law. It was not so in the beginning, so it was obviously the idea of God that man would always stop to reflect, to acknowledge, to remember to celebrate, to rest. However, when His creation proved otherwise, it suffered a fall, and laws had to be put in place to protect man from himself. Without this law, man self-destructs. He steals life off of the back end of his life and never sees it coming.

Lee Bueno-Aguer in Fast Your Way To Health, talks about the therapeutic side of fasting. She said this:

"Fasting simply provides ideal conditions for the body to regenerate, repair and rejuvenate itself...By abstaining from and taking only water, you relieve your body of digesting and eliminating a constant intake of food. Our bodies finally catch up, respond to rest, and use the energy for healing and rejuvenation. Fasting provides the ideal conditions for the body to rejuvenate itself as the toxic buildup decreases day by day. Rest alone—even without fasting—will increase the elimination, although not nearly to the same extent.[26]

Again, we see the underestimated, rarely discussed need for the inner body, to rest. One physician mentioned that the digestive system is extremely worked daily and when it is not functioning at its highest capability, toxins from foods are not properly discarded. Like any of the other muscles or organs in the body, it needs rest. How often do we eat something just before bed? Even at night, our digestive tract is at work. Fasting gives that vitally important body part a time to heal.

---

[26] Lee Bueno-Aguer, *Fast Your Way To Health*, Whitaker House, New Kensington, PA, 1991, pg 94

Wayne Muller said, *"...during Sabbath the Jews, by keeping sacred rest, could maintain their spiritual ground wherever they were, even in protected exile from their own country. It was not Israel that kept the Sabbath, it is said, but the Sabbath kept Israel."*[27] I am convinced of the veracity of that statement. Often we see things like fasting, going to church, keeping the Sabbath, setting a time early to pray/study, as a necessary burden. Yet if we understand their end result we could not categorize them as burdens but necessary means to the God kind of life (life more abundant). Sabbaths will keep us, if we will keep them. Sabbaths, rests or reflection days will not only extend our lives, but enhance the quality of that extended time.

I spoke to a young man about eliminating tobacco from his daily routine and his response was that his grandmother smoked and lived eighty odd years. My response was/is three-fold. One, her eating habits and the ingredients or toxins in food today are different, thereby lengthening shelf times at the grocery stores, but shortening our life span. Secondly, she may have lived eighty plus years and that is good, but what is eighty years if fifteen (15) of them are in poor health? Lastly, maybe she was suppose to live 100 years or more in great health, and see and affect several (at least one more) generation, but died before her time because she smoked tobacco. She could have used a fast as a Sabbath to see her future, leaving behind anything that would hinder her from arriving there in the time and condition God desired her to.

Get it in your beautiful brain. Your body needs a break every now and then. When I was a college student, I hung out with the guys who were in church and out of church. I had been brought up in church, but didn't have a revelation of "sonship", never heard the scripture that my body was the temple of the Holy Spirit. I drank extensively and experimented with <u>some</u> drugs. I was a strange guy though. Every so often, I would quit

---

[27] Wayne Muller, *Sabbath*, Bantham Books, New York, NY, 1999, pg 9

for a week or so to make sure I could. I wanted to make sure I was not getting addicted to anything. I think back on that now and thank God on one hand, because that must have been Him. On the other hand, I wonder how I made it or why would anyone want to chance becoming addicted to drugs and alcohol? Nobody, I suppose wants to, but if you start to use them, you give yourself an opportunity for addiction. We addressed addictions in Chapter 5. They can be broken. One addiction is to food. Believe me when I say, I am a client of what I write about. Cookies, pound cake (homemade), popcorn with butter (stove top popped) are things I have to carefully use Sabbaths and extended fasts to make sure they do not become addictions. The society we live in is carb-centered. Bad carbohydrates are dangerous to the health and as addictive as any alcohol, drug, tobacco or caffeine. They feed several physical deficiencies.

    I used to have a problem with gout (ouch). It is painful to say the word. It is much more painful to experience it. I went to my personal physician and he told me I had the "rich man's disease". I was anxious to know why being rich was so painful because I was ready to denounce any part of it. I said to myself, if money caused that much pain, you could have it. He was referring to the ability to purchase foods that most people who are poor could not (regularly). He gave me some little pills (colchine) and pain killers (hallelujah). Now I must admit that I am not the pill taking guy. It must be an absolute necessity for me to take medication (not vitamins/supplements). This was necessity! I could no longer bear the pain. I went through this several times before I received a revelation. Why not seek a naturopathic doctor and discover the root cause instead of medicating this for life. I researched gout, found out everything that caused the flaring up of uric acid to be stored in your joints and I eliminated them from my diet. It took some fasting to overcome some things I had an affinity for, but I must admit that the pain helped as much as the fasting. I do know people who have continued eating the same way and just suffering it to be so, while they carry those little pills and pain killers everywhere they go. I call them weak, but that's my opinion. Here we are, the smartest creatures on earth. Here we are, having dominion over all things in the earth, but we cannot overcome crabmeat. Is that insane or not? How could I allow ice cream, peanuts, lobster, alcohol etc. to beat me and control me? Do you get it yet?

You see, a Sabbath is a testing period. You will see what calls you to it and makes you desire it more than normal. That thing has power and needs your attention to overcome it. Most physical problems surface because of diets that are poorly managed. Dr. Rex Russell said:

"People can become addicted to foods. Common examples of this are dependencies on caffeine, fat, sugar and salt. We can also overdo and become addicted to food God gave for our use. In Deuteronomy 32:13-14, God discusses several foods He has provided for us. Then in verse 15 He charges: Jeshurun grew fat and kicked; filled with food, he became heavy and sleek. He abandoned the God who made him and rejected the Rock his Savior. "Jeshurun" means the "upright one," and refers to God's people, Israel. God's own people had forsaken Him, substituting Him an overabundance of food that made them sluggish from gluttony. They were "hooked on food." Both acute and chronic conditions can result from any kind of overconsumption." [28]

This is not just about food. It is also about the liquids we consume. When Cherral Moore; one of my beloved parishioners was diagnosed with cancer, we went on an extensive research to tackle this (after laying hands on her and believing God for healing). To my discovery (Google Dr.

---

[28] Rex Russell, *What the Bible Says About Healthy Living*, Regal Books, Ventura CA,1983, pg 35

Larraine Day), I found that even coffee is not good to drink when trying to overcome diseases. It helps dry the system out. It was then that I began to read about the best drink on the planet. Most children do not drink it. Many adults do not like its taste. It is not sweet enough or tingly enough. It is called, water. My doctor asked me years ago what I washed my body with. I told him soap and water. He said surprisingly, "You don't use Coke, Pepsi, Tea, alcoholic beverages, etc?" I said, "of course not, that is silly." He then offered this brilliant medical observation. Why do you wash the inside of your body with it then? If you really want to understand how much the body needs water and why it is so vital to your health, go on the internet or to a book store and look up F. Batmanghelidj, M.D. or www.watercure.com. He wrote a book entitled, *Your Body's Many Cries For Water*, which is a medical breakthrough. He indicates that many people with physical complications are not sick, just thirsty. You also need a Sabbath from liquids. Flush, cleanse and wash your insides. Replenish your brain (which is over 80% water). You will need that brain sometime today.

Before we move on to Chapter 8, let me leave you with five (5) things you should do when you see fasting as a Sabbath.

A Sabbath should cause you to do each one of these, some of which we have mentioned already but will serve as a reminder:

(1) Reassessment – Where are you now? Where should you be? How do you get to where you want to go? Are there any stumbling blocks to your goals?

(2) Reflection – Are my actions pleasing God? Am I saying about my work the same thing I hear the Father saying about His? He said, "it was good." What am I doing that does not line up with the Word? This should be a daily practice, but every seven days is better than not at all.

(3) Re-imaging – you were made in the image of God. As you look at your life this is the correction stage. Every

seven (7) days you should take a day out to re-image yourself. You should take time out to allow God to speak to every area of your life that is out of synch with His purpose for you. You cannot do this without world detoxification and Word intoxication.

(4) Reconciliation – this part of Sabbath is for you to look at every relationship in your life and begin to right the wrongs in them by faith, not feelings. Use the Word of God, counseling, prayer, Christian writings, etc., whatever it takes. Get those relationships healed, healthy and whole. Unhealthy, unattended relationships in your life cause you to operate at less than full potential. Stress slows the ability to achieve your best. Your marriage, your parenting, your boss – employee relationship, your friendships, your enemies, people of other cultures, should all be looked at as an opportunity to reconcile.

II Corinthians 5:18 says, *"[18]All this is from God, who reconciled us to himself through Christ and gave us the ministry of reconciliation..."* Fasting is a time of reconciliation. I John 4:20 says, *"[20]If anyone says, "I love God," yet hates his brother, he is a liar. For anyone who does not love his brother, whom he has seen, cannot love God, whom he has not seen."*

Remember Matthew 6:9? It begins the model prayer, which begins with "Our Father." Our denotes that we are of one family, the human family. One race of people are we, human, even though we may have many colors. If you go to India, in different parts of the country, there are all types of people, shades and sizes that make up the land, dark, light, tall, short, slanted eyed (near the Burmese boarder in the Nagaland). The same is true in other countries, Cuba for example. They are nevertheless all Indian people or all Cuban. Many colors one race is a mentality America would do well to adopt.

Finally:

(5) Rest, Restoration, Refreshment – which is for the mind as well as the physical body. The mind and body need a

Sabbath. Rest is a necessity for long life. The alternative is burn-out and/or, as we mentioned earlier, retirement via stroke, heart attack or other diseases which attach themselves to broken down bodies.

Every seven (7) days take a day to give your body a rest. If you cannot do it every seven days, then do it when a fast is called in your ministry, but for the sake of your health (physically and spiritually), do it. Remember this important point that is worth repeating, "Life comes off of the back end, not the front." What you do or do not do for your health today, will catch up with you later, when you cannot see it coming. That leads me right into the next chapter. No matter how you start fasting, start. The goal is not to let it be always parented by others. At some point, you must begin to fast on your own, because you see the need in your life, your families, your city or your ministry. It's called a "fasted life". Let's go further.

10
For Tradition or Triumph: Lent or Life-Style

> *Zechariah 8:18-19 – "^{18}Again the word of the LORD Almighty came to me. ^{19}This is what the LORD Almighty says: "The fasts of the fourth, fifth, seventh and tenth months will become joyful and glad occasions and happy festivals for Judah. Therefore love truth and peace."*
>
> *Mark 9:29 {KJV} – "^{29}And he said unto them, this kind can come forth by nothing, but by prayer and fasting."*

Have you ever noticed how every year when lent comes around, that even the most marginal church attendee talks about what they are giving up for lent? Even unbelievers are trying it. It always reminds me of New Year's Eve service. People spend time talking about what they are going to be giving up in the New Year or are busy making New Year resolutions. Many people sense the need to return to church, get a membership at the gym, hire a physical trainer, quit smoking, and/or a host of other things. The beginning of the year is full of promises. Yet, "the race is not given to the swift, nor the battle to the strong, but to he that endures to the end". Lent has become a popular season for the retail moguls, leading to the spring-time's mini-Christmas, which we call Easter.

My uncle Michael and his friends usually celebrate lent by giving up drinking for 40 days. Even if they meet at the lounge (Chicago terminology for a bar), they drink water or pop (soda). It is quite an amazing thing to see when you have been around long enough to notice how much and how often they spend time drinking. I was my uncle's protégé in baseball, girls and how to handle my liquor. Thank God for deliverance from games, girls (one is enough for me – my wife) and guzzling.

It was an amazing thing being in that environment, where consumption was an art form, and then seeing them move to the place of complete abstinence. I had to witness it to see that they were able to do it. When my uncle told me he had quit smoking (I never asked if it was a result of lent), I was amazed. Then, lent ended, and the celebration of sobriety erupted Easter Sunday night. The cigarettes never returned, but the glasses were toasting again. They spent 40 days clean, safe and toxic free, and then returned to form when lent ended.

They took a Sabbath. They gave their bodies a break, which on the one hand was good. On the other hand, they missed the point of the season. I know this because I missed it for years as well. The point of the time of lent is to release something to God for life, not just a season. It is to teach the body to live toxic free. To *rid* itself of poison, not just to relieve it. Anything hindering the ears to hear the voice of God over every other voice is dangerous and destructive. Tradition calls for a fast as a ritual or religious practice. What we need is a relationship changing fast. A relationship changing fast is the type that is focused on altering our relationship with God. It challenges us to clear or cleanse anything from our lives that hinder triumph over worldly behavior defined in scripture. It draws us nearer to Him.

Again I say, fasting for Christians is not about our religion. It is about our relationship with God. It is about conforming to the image of our Father. Hebrews 1:3 says this:

> "*³The Son is the radiance of God's glory and the exact representation of his being, sustaining all things by his powerful word. After he had provided purification for sins, he sat down at the right hand of the Majesty in heaven.*"

This is the aim of every Christians, to be the radiance of the Father's glory. We should long to be the exact representation of His being. This takes place during the process of re-imaging, which fasting is our master teacher.

Zechariah 8:18-19 says:

> "*¹⁸Again the word of the LORD Almighty came to me. ¹⁹This is what the LORD Almighty says: "The fasts of the fourth, fifth, seventh and tenth months will become joyful and glad occasions and happy festivals for Judah. Therefore love truth and peace."*"

As you read these verses, you get the distinct impression that fasting, in order to be affective should be done often. It is not about *Lent*. It is a life-style. It is not about tradition. It is about living a triumphant life so that the world has a model of what Christ looks like in the flesh. This is their only hope for salvation. You are the only Jesus some people will ever see. Their eternity rests in your ability to model Him before them. Notice that Zechariah says there was a fast in the fourth, fifth, seventh and tenth months and that they would be joyful or glad occasions, not sad, painful ones. This is life-style fasting. The fasted life produces joy, gladness, peace and wholeness. Reading Mark 9:29 {KJV}, "*²⁹And he said unto them, This kind can come forth by nothing, but by prayer and fasting*", we see how Jesus felt about the power of a fasted life. He told the disciples that there would be some victories they would never experience without fasting. There are some realms of authority unattainable without fasting and praying.

Lent was never supposed to be a ritualistic event anyway. Lent was intended as a time of preparation for the resurrection, return of the bridegroom. That would mean that the bride should be preparing for the wedding day. Have you read the story of Esther lately? We get so fascinated with *her* story that we miss the story of her predecessor, Vashti. Queen Vashti is a necessary study. The king called her to come to where he was. Granted, the king had grown intoxicated by the spirits he was drinking, but it was still not Vashti's place to ignore him, or refuse to come when he called. She became caught up in how she was treated and forgot who *she* was. More importantly, she forgot who *he* was. She was not to be held responsible for his actions. She was however held accountable for her own. Her flesh controlled her, and put her in position to lose her anointed position, her authority, her place ruling beside the king. When she allowed her flesh to rule her, it resulted in her excommunication. She was cut off from the pleasures of royalty.

Now enters a new era in the kingdom. The search goes out for another Queen. Vashti is forgotten. Her name is never to be spoken in the palace without it being associated with disgrace or shame. Esther emerges from obscurity. She takes a year bathing, beautifying and cultivating herself. She takes this season of her life to learn what pleases and what doesn't please the king, before she has the opportunity to enter his presence and become the new bride. Patience, persistence, passion, pain, denial of self and attention to detail all had to be hers to become the choice as bride-queen for the king, the bridegroom. This is the portrait of fasting. Preparing for the life I am going to live with the king. Fasting is my preparation ground. I am an unlikely candidate. My history says that I am a foreigner, but my preparation says choose me. My background says that I have not associated with the right crowd, but my commitment to bathe and soak to get the stench of the world off of me, interests the King and makes Him desire me as a worthwhile investment. Fasting is that bathing, cleansing, preparation time that brings pleasure to the King and me. I even feel better about coming into His presence.

Fasting begins with an inspection of the inner man. In the previous chapter, we labeled it reassignment. It recognizes that my inner man has a shadow or reflection that is called, my outer man. My behavior is a reflection of my attitude. To change it, reprogramming is required. When the bible says in Matthew 12:34 {KJV}, *"...out of the abundance of the heart the mouth speaketh"*, it causes us to make considerations daily about what we allow to enter our hearts though our ear gates. Who speaks into your life most? You *are* what you hang around. You will return what is deposited in you. Zig Zigler says, *"How you think determines what you become."*[29] Don't let your thinking be dominated by people who do not have Christ as Lord of their lives. If you do, you will always live with impaired vision and an unrestrained tongue, guided by a contaminated heart. Listen dear friend, you may be a candidate for an extreme makeover. It is okay. You will not be the first or the last.

When you inspect your inner man, the you that makes you who you are, note the things that are inside of you that do not look like your heavenly Father. Again, do I look like Him in word and deed? Do I think like Him? Do I see things the same way He sees things? Am I participating in the promotion of the family business? Or am I busy with my own agenda? Is *this* world more important than eternity? What is my world-view? These are the questions we must raise in our lives. Do I live with a biblical world-view? Do I have any character traits that need corrective surgery? If I have any, today is a good day to correct them. What do I need to do to face my flaws?

---

[29] Zig Zigler, *See You At The Top*, Pelican Publishing, Gretna, LA, 1977, pg 206

Facing Your Flaws: My 4 Step Process

Be careful here. This section may be hazardous to your ego. If your feelings are touchy feely, then brace yourself.

1. **Ask yourself** (comparing yourself to scripture, not comparing yourself to others) what do you see as flaws in your life? Get a notebook. Write down all your qualities and characteristics you see as, "Caution, God at Work Zone". Now, you may need to write an, "I'm Okay" list first, if it will help you feel better. But wait, its not over yet. I said *four* steps.

2. **Ask your family and friends** (a few honest ones). A true friend will tell you what they see in you. The problem is, many people do not have true friends. If we did, we would be working on ourselves consistently. Do you have any family and/or friends you can ask? Are you too sensitive to receive their honesty? Is that a flesh issue? If they tell you the truth, can you handle it? If you cannot, then you will never be free. Have you ever heard, "the truth shall set you or make you free (John 8:32)?" We often live flawed lives, even as Christians, because we will not receive constructive criticism.

3. **Ask a co-worker**. Sometimes people we work with observe us, but never are close enough to us to tell us things about us that would help us. They just work with us and consider our lives none of their business. They do not get paid to help, repair or correct our sub-standard ways. They would rather not deal with the tension that comes with calling attention to the difference between, who we say we

are, and how we act. They may be better suited to discuss or at least listen to those things about us when they are said outside of our presence (behind our back). They do not dislike us, but they would rather not deal with the consequences of confrontation.

Tell one or two of them you are doing a spiritual survey of your personality traits and work effort and that you would like for them to honestly give you an analysis. Tell them they do not have to sign their name, but give them some idea of what areas to address. If they type it, tell them where to send it, especially if they prefer it to be anonymous. Express to them how much it is going to help you truly become a better person as well as a better Christian.

4. **Ask an enemy**. If you know someone who does not really like you, ask them to tell you why (without being defensive). You should pray before you do this! Ask a Christian and an unbeliever. Find out if their statements match. This is probably the most important level, other than your family. Your family is important because they see you at your worst or at your relaxed self. There are no unintentional put-ons with them. Sometimes at work and other places, we can become a little different because of expectations, but not at home. On the other hand, with people, whom we know do not like us, it may be one of two things. We do not *care* (which needs to be addressed by you sometime soon) or we care and we overdo trying to impress upon them why they should like us, to the point where we are not genuine.

Everyone has character flaws. Today is as good a day as any to get free from yours. The question is, will you make the effort? Have you considered the greatest good that could surface from this exercise? That great good is, that you might win some people to Christ. That great good could be that enemies become friends and Satan would lose ground as he watches love rise from ashes.

You Can't Afford to Wait For Lent to "Loose it and Let it go"

Whatever your discoveries are from the above exercise cannot wait for a season on the calendar before they get fixed. Tradition says, "Lent is the season to fast". That works out well if you are only a week or two away from lent, but what if it is July when the discoveries are made? Are you going to wait eight (8) months before you deal with whatever maybe crippling you (even if you have not seen the end result of the crippling yet)? I know it's hard to hear crippling without seeing wheelchair or bedridden state. However, in Luke 13, the bible records a woman bent over by a "spirit of infirmity". It was not a physical ailment or disease of the blood or bones, but of the emotions, that did not allow her to walk as she should as a daughter of Abraham (a daughter of faith), which positions her to have rights to the life of blessings.

You could die or break down completely waiting for lent to appear. Lent begins whenever there is a ***need*** for you to get prepared for the bridegroom. It is not a calendar time; it is a spiritual season of preparation for resurrection. Demonic spirits do not care what calendar season it is. They just want you dead. Fasting cannot be reserved for the calendar season of lent, it must be a lifestyle.

M. Scott Peck, M.D., says:
"The more clearly we see the reality of the world, the better equipped we are to deal with the world. The less clearly we see the reality of

the world—the more our minds are befuddled by falsehood, misperceptions and illusions—the less able we will be to determine correct courses of action and make wise decisions. Our view of reality is like a map with which to negotiate the terrain of life. If the map is true and accurate, we will generally know where we are, and if we have decided where we want to go, we will generally know how to get there. If the map is false and inaccurate, we generally will be lost.

While this is obvious, it is something that most people to a greater or lesser degree choose to ignore. They ignore it because our route to reality is not easy. First of all, we are not born with maps; we have to make them, and the making requires effort. The more effort we make to appreciate and perceive reality, the larger and more accurate our maps will be. But many do not want to make this effort." [30]

Fasting is one of the avenues to take to help you get on the right road to the person you were born to be. Beginning that road is never easy, but the alternative is infinitely more disturbing. Are you weary of missing the mark? Tired of destiny detours? Puzzled by cloudy visions on the road to promises? Then make the effort to position yourself to receive clear instructions.

Its Over When You Win

Tradition says that a fast is over when 21 or 40 days are over. It says, when lent ends, the fast is over. However, I want to suggest to you that a fast should be guided by what I call, "The Jacob Rule". In Genesis 32:24-30 the bible records that Jacob wrestled with an angel. He was told by the angel to let

---

[30] M. Scott Peck, M.D., *The Road Less Traveled*, Simon & Schuster Inc., New York, NY, 1978, pg 44

him go. Jacob responded with this, *"I will not let you go until you bless me* (verse 26)." You should not come out of a fast until what you went in with, is broken. Whatever malady that took you to the fast must be defeated before you come out. This is not about *tradition*. It is about **TRIUMPH**! That is why fasting must be a lifestyle. The fasted life will keep every rising fleshly desire under submission and cause you to live a triumphant life. Over every enemy or inner me invasion, the new you will have a loud voice crying out, "It is Written".

Remember this one important thing. A dead man cannot be invaded by the enemy. Satan feeds on unholy things in you. If it is dead, he has nothing to eat at you. He must leave you for a season and hope to come back when there is a challenge you are facing, like whether you want to die so you can save someone else. He is after your will. He desires your decisions to be made in his favor. He is always recruiting. Why not? He knows where the most powerful soldiers in the world are. They are in God's family (army). God's army is the triumphant one. Read the end of the story (the book of Revelations) and you will see the outcome. The question is very simple my friend. "Are you going to be on the winning team?" Whatever you do, make up your mind that you will not leave this life a loser. What a long, long time you will have to think about the consequences of that decision. Well, to put it plainly, you will have eternity to contemplate it. Why not make up your mind now, and help convince everyone you know to do the same. Do not leave one family member, friend or foe behind. Eternity is too long to be filled with regret.

I leave you with this, as we journey on to Chapter 11 (Kingdom Consciousness: Your New Beginning), I John 4:4-5 says, *"[4]for everyone born of God overcomes the world. This is the victory that has overcome the world, even our faith. [5]Who is it that overcomes the world? Only he who believes that Jesus is the Son of God."*

So my dear friend, I call you filled with FAITH. YOU ARE A BELIEVER! Say that, I AM A BELIEVER! Jesus is the Son of God, therefore, I AM A WORLD OVERCOMER, HALLELUJAH! Now let's go take some take some ground for the King and the Kingdom.

11
Kingdom Consciousness: My New Beginning

> *"Fasting is the soul of prayer; mercy is the lifeblood of fasting. So, if you pray, fast; if you fast, show mercy. If you want your petition to be heard, hear the petition of others. If you do not close your ear to other, you open God's ear to yourself."*
> *-Saint Peter Chrysologus (c.380–c. 450; Doctor of the Catholic*

How different it is for Western culture to grasp the full meaning of this very important word, Kingdom. Too often, it fades into the shadow of the other words in the sentence. Yet, it does not belong in obscurity, but in plain view. The gospel of Mark is said to be written first the four gospel accounts. Mark begins in chapter one by expressing to us the agenda and focal point of the life of Jesus. He sets His priorities. It is to fast and pray, preach the Kingdom, and to cast out demons.

It is the fasting and praying that enabled Jesus to do the later two. It is the fasting and praying that opens ones eyes to see the kingdom. We cannot preach what we cannot see. Otherwise, our preaching or teaching whether you are assigned as a corporate (church/pastor) or individual Christian who ministers has little or no attraction. A revelation of that, which we are preaching, is necessary to give us passion about which we are talking. People who talk about subjects in which they themselves are not fully persuaded, are rarely persuasive in getting people to follow them. Fasting finds success in you when you focus on certain areas to study while you are fasting.

I want to suggest to you to see clearly that Jesus preached and lived kingdom. If that be the case, then kingdom must be *an* area if not *the* area of primary concern for us as His disciples. As a matter of fact, without an understanding of kingdom, it is very likely that we will lose our way often and find ourselves with self-centered or other people-centered agendas.

If fasting is meant to break my will so that I can commit to concentrating on His, then let's do it, so we can represent Him in all we say and do. Do you not believe that it is time to declare that you have the mind of Christ? It should be your earnest desire to think like Jesus every moment you live in the earth. Why, because the kingdom of God is always at hand. Somebody is doing and is preparing, whether they like it or not, to face the King of Kings. You and I are on the preparation team. It is our assignment to direct our lost brothers and sisters back to the family. Didn't Dad say that He desired that none would perish, but that all would come into the knowledge of the truth (II Peter 3:9)?

Naves Topical Bible says that the Kingdom of God is:
"The sovereign rule of God manifested in Christ to defeat His enemies, creating a people over whom He reigns, and issuing in a realm or realms in which the power of His reign is experienced. All they are members of the kingdom of God who voluntarily submit to the rule of God in their lives. Entrance into the kingdom is by the new birth (John 3:3-5); two stages in the kingdom of God; present and future in an eschatological sense; Jesus said that his ability to cast out demons was evidence

that the kingdom of God had come among men (Matthew 12:28)." [31]

Note the last statement, where it indicates that it is the ability to cast out demons that evidenced the kingdom of God. If that be the case, is much of the church today missing their kingdom assignment? I must admit, until recent years I did not hear much talk about "the kingdom of God". The emphasis in the churches I grew up in was on preaching, not much teaching on these areas. We did have Sunday School lessons, but no in depth study on vital doctrinal issues. The deep treasures of holiness, nature of God, righteous living, kingdom principles, fasting, casting out demons, the purpose of angels, how to pray, what to pray for guarding your tongue etc. baptism of the Holy Spirit, were not expanded upon.

How could Jesus maintain the kingdom of God or the kingdom of heaven so much and it not be of supreme interest to us? It is mentioned some seventy (70) times in the four gospels. Once is enough to call our attention to it, but seventy times? Sixty-nine of those times are in the first three gospels. While John only uses the term once, he does use another phrase with the same kind of meaning ("eternal life"). Jon Sanford, in his book, The Kingdom Within, notes, that when Jesus kept saying to the disciples that the kingdom of God was <u>like</u> so and so, that it was done for the world to pay attention. The disciples close contact with Jesus helped them grasp an understanding of the other world things, but the multitudes needed parables or illustrations to open their eyes. They need a revelation of a new order. They obviously were more aware of kings and kingdoms than we are today (especially those who live in the Western Hemisphere), but still they needed revelation of the kingdom over all kingdoms and the King of all Kings. Sanford writes:

> *"This is why Jesus calls the kingdom 'a mystery'. The Greek word for this is mysterion. A "mysterion" was something to be known, but*

---

[31] NIV Naves Topical Bible, Zondervan Publishing House, Grand Rapids MI, 1994, pg 600

it was an initiated knowledge, knowledge that person could acquire only through his or her own individual insight and experienced that could not be communicated through an ordinary educational process."[32]

That has revelation written all over it. Therefore, if fasting cause's revelation to happen, and you need a revelation of the kingdom; then a sure path to that revelation is through fasting.

This chapter is designed to give you a start in your desire to understand more about the kingdom of God, which Jesus said is within you. If it is within you then it is available anytime you want to grasp it. You are always close to the understanding of who you are, where you come from and why you are here. You just need your eyes open to see it. It is the job of the Holy Spirit to open your eyes. It is your job to seek Him and His guidance. Intimacy escorts you into the revelation realm. It is possible to live all of your life without a clear understanding of your purpose. To live your whole life accidently bumping into it and experiencing moments of supernatural clarity and bliss, never knowing that you could have and should have had this as an ongoing experience.

Understanding the kingdom is the key you need that will unlock the door to your purpose. Your purpose being fulfilled is the key to the door that leads to the abundant life. That door entrance does not exclude you from experiencing things that other human beings experience. It merely helps you see them differently. At times it will help you see them coming so you can prepare for them. At other times it will help you use them as a ministry to others. Always, you will see things working together for your good and the good of those who love God and are "called according to His purpose". The abundant life is therefore not merely consisting of worldly possessions as some who have taken the prosperity message to solely mean

---

[32] John Sanford, *The Kingdom Within,* Harpers Row, San Francisco, CA, 1970, Rev 1987, pg 29

money. It is "Shalom" a peace "that passes understanding". It is seeing life from God's eyes. That I am content wherever I am, even in the not yet having received the promises stage. In expectations I am not angry or anxious. Even if my delay is not until I get to my faith assigned destination, I am okay with that.

Truly, I do expect what I can handle in my flesh. If I can handle riches or financial wealth, with integrity, and use it to glorify God and advance the kingdom here in the earth, then I welcome it. If the Father sees it will make me stumble out of favor with Him, then I want Him to keep it and entrust it in the hands of the perfect steward. I never desire to be a stumbling block for one (more) person to see Jesus. That, my dear friend, is the aftermath of a fasted life and the heart of a former "I am going to be a millionaire", for no reason, person. Deuteronomy 8:18 says this, *"[18] But remember the LORD your God, for it is he who gives you the ability to produce wealth, and so confirms his covenant, which he swore to your forefathers, as it is today."* It is His covenant, His work on the earth that I am here to establish, not my own.

The kingdom within, as you get a clear understanding, is suppose to produce kingdom living without. Once I understand that I am a seed of God, I then produce what is in me.

You must begin to have a clear understanding of the kingdom. You must know the King and have a revelation of His "Dom" (dominion). Dr. Myles Monroe does an excellent job in his book Rediscovering the Kingdom, breaking down the kingdom concept. What an advantage he had, growing up in a society that used this concept in its form of government. American Christianity could learn much from this study. He mentions the commonality of all kingdom components and defines them so that the reader may be clear on what Jesus is referring to when He mentions kingdom. There are ten (10) basic components that kingdoms have. He says, "all kingdoms have:

- *A King and Lord – authority flows from the king and the word of the king is supreme.*

- *A Territory – the domain over which the king experiences total authority. The territory and its resources and people are all personal property of the king. The king by right owns all and therefore, is considered Lord over all.*

- *A Constitution – the covenant of a king with his citizenry and expresses the mind and will of the king for his citizens and the kingdom. It contains the benefits and privileges of the kingdom. (The bible contains this for the Kingdom of God.)*

- *A Citizenry – the people that live under the rule of the king. Citizenship is not a right but a privilege and is a result of the king's choice. Once one becomes a citizen of the kingdom, all the rights of citizenship are at the citizen's pleasure.*

- *Laws – acceptable principles established by the king himself, by which his kingdom will function and be administered. The laws are the way by which one is guaranteed access to benefits. Violations of laws place one at odds with the king and interrupt ones favorable position with him.*

- *Privileges – benefits which the faithful citizens receive.*

- *A Code of Ethics – the acceptable conduct expected of the kingdom citizens: moral standards, social relationships, attitude, etc.*

- *An Army – the security system for citizen protection.*

- *A Commonwealth – the economic system which guarantees each citizen equal access to financial security. All citizens share the wealth of the kingdom.*

- *A Social Culture – the life and mannerisms of the king and his citizens that make them different or separates them from all others around them."* [33]

As you read each of these ten basic components of a kingdom you should see or begin to see yourself operating as a part of <u>the</u> greatest kingdom. The kingdom of God is that kingdom. Begin to understand then, how your life is suppose to fit into every one of those ten basic areas. For instance, how do you see Jesus? Do you see Him as King, Lord of your life? Is He the supreme authority over your life? I mean, is His word final, no question, no doubts, no hesitation of obedience? Does He have all right to speak concerning all of your affairs? Is your property His property? Is your house, car, family, money, time and talent His? Is the bible your constitution? Do you use it as your guide for living? For giving? For forgiving? Is His word your words? Do you believe that you have all the rights and benefits of His kingdom? Do you fight battles according to kingdom rules? Do you summon angelic help to involve them in battles? Do you believe in God's financial system: tithing, offerings, seedtime, harvest, lending to the poor, that none should have need in the body? Do you live with distinctiveness from the world's culture? Are you a world overcomer? Are people drawn to the king and His kingdom because of you?

To position yourself for a yes to all of these questions you will have to first be born again and see yourself differently

---

[33] Myles Monroe, *Rediscovering the Kingdom, Ancient Hope for Our 21st Century World,* Destiny Image, Shippensburg, PA, 2004, pg 64-67

than you ever have before. I am not talking about baptism in a pool of water and a giving of one's hand to a minister during a ceremonial right-hand of fellowship. I mean truly looking at the life of Jesus and asking the father to make you just like Him. Completely breaking every tie to making choices based upon my world, secular trained, parental modeled, academically prepared, perspective. Now, I am only using all these things in light of how the King desires me to use them. I no longer live in this world only. I live in two worlds. I exist in one to live eternally in another. I am on an assignment in one, representing another.

When you come to this revelation, some people will think you are crazy. They will taunt, tease, write you off as gone overboard. If you read the Gospels and the books of Acts, you will see that is what happened to the disciples and apostles. It was done to them by people who were supposedly religious. They claimed to know God, but couldn't recognize Him in the flesh. Some of them were religious enough to fast twice a week, but still could not see. Why? Because there are some things you cannot do while fasting. Isaiah 58 helps us with this, as well as Jeremiah 14:12 – *"[12] Although they fast, I will not listen to their cry; though they offer burnt offerings and grain offerings, I will not accept them. Instead, I will destroy them with the sword, famine and plague."*. God does not receive certain kinds of fasting. You cannot fast and do as you choose. A fast is designed to open your eyes to see life from God's eyes. It is to see yourself as a love vessel, to relate to others as siblings not statues to be worshipped or even constantly saluted. Saluting may be offered to positions of authority, but they are saluted not because of superiority, but as an honor for service. Leaders need to fast often so they do not allow any room for ego and idolatry to enter, thereby having the inner me becoming their worst enemy.

Fasting is supposed to produce thanksgiving for the privilege to be chosen by the king. Yet, thanksgiving sounds too once a yearish. It reminds me of why I have mixed emotions during the Thanksgiving and Christmas season. The world always seems to be at its best then. Celebrations are at an all time high. Cultures rarely clash. Social order is sweet. Yet January finds us returning to normal. Why? Because these seasons are social events not celebrated lifestyles. Fasting should lead us beyond thanksgiving to the realm of "thanksliving". It should lead us from Christmas holidays to, "Jesus born in me everyday". This is Kingdom Consciousness. I am an ambassador for the King.

When I see myself as an ambassador, I see myself as living here on an assignment to represent the ideals of the King only. I have His interest at heart in everything I say and do. When I sense I am wavering in any way, I have to do something to position myself back to that posture. Fasting and praying are the answers. I must be careful always. I must stay in tune with my King. He depends on me to say what He says and do as He would do, so that the world where I've been assigned gets His message clearly. My opinion doesn't matter. My feelings are a mute issue. I must keep them under subjection or I could ruin the opportunity for people to travel to my country. When people see me, I want them to say, "you look like the King!"

You must see yourself as an ambassador everywhere you are and in whatever you are doing. You can never look at your job, what you wear to work, or who you are supervised by, as an excuse for why you are not functioning in your office. You are not defined by position, income, clothing or educational achievements. Whether a sanitation worker or scientist, street sweeper or senator, librarian or law clerk, attorney or administrative assistant, maid or mailman, teacher or student, cook/chef or CEO, physician or paperboy, if you are a Christian your assignment is to be an AMBASSADOR. You are eternally more important than your worldly hired position. There is great worth in you. Peoples' eternity hinge on your ability to know who you are and stay focused on your assignment. When you enter a room, the atmosphere changes.

The fragrance is altered. Anointing is the new smell that permeates the room. Royalty has just arrived. The King's own family is present. As a matter of fact, when you are there, The King is There! People are now being pointed to a higher calling in life. They are being led towards love, peace, unselfishness and holiness. They are being led towards purpose.

Ken Hemphill, whose writings on the Kingdom of God are insightful and inspiring, begins the final chapter of his book Empowering Kingdom Growth The Heartbeat of God, by telling the story of one of his favorite childhood characters (who happens to be mine as well). He writes, "As a young lad, I was always fascinated with the story of Robin Hood, amazed by his exploits and his ability with a bow and arrow. I remember as a kid trying to duplicate his feats …with little success.

But the plot running behind this familiar story was the delayed return of King Richard. In his absence evil men had taken control of the government and were squandering the resources of the kingdom, behaving as if he would never return. Robin Hood, on the other hand—through all of his remarkable adventures—was working from a totally different perspective. He was always bravely laboring in the light of the return of England's rightful king.

I'm sure you see the parallel.

Just as in the story of Robin Hood, we Christians labor for a King who is now physically absent from the earth. And— just like Robin Hood's contemporaries—many people today are squandering the King's resources, living as if he were never coming back.

But our King *will* return! His kingdom *is* coming! And if we hope to experience this kingdom in the midst of our daily lives, we must live in the light of this fundamental truth. We must live as if we really believe it." [34]

---

[34] Ken Hemphill, *Empowering Kingdom Growth EKG The Heartbeat of God,* Broadman & Holman Publishers, Nashville, TN, 2004, pg 282-283

As we close this chapter, take an opportunity to look at these parables. Ask God for revelation on each of them. As a matter of fact, while you are fasting, take each one daily, as your food for thought. Make a decision today to read Ken Hemphill's book, Empowering Kingdom Growth EKG The Heartbeat of God, as well as Myles Monroe's Rediscovering the Kingdom and John Sanford's The Kingdom Within. If you will do this over the next 90 days, you will completely transform your life.

Matthew 13:44 says this, *"^{44}"The kingdom of heaven is like treasure hidden in a field. When a man found it, he hid it again, and then in his joy went and sold all he had and bought that field."* Now, are you willing to sell everything (not necessarily literally)? Are you willing to sell out? Do you recognize yet, that this treasure you have in Christ is more valuable than anything else in the world and worth giving up everything else so you can acquire it? Like the rich young ruler, and like Abraham, God doesn't really want your stuff, He just wants to know that it is available as His to use as He pleases.

Parables about the Kingdom

1. Matthew 13:31-33 – *"^{31}He told them another parable: "The kingdom of heaven is like a mustard seed, which a man took and planted in his field. ^{32}Though it is the smallest of all your seeds, yet when it grows, it is the largest of garden plants and becomes a tree, so that the birds of the air come and perch in its branches."*

   ^{33}*He told them still another parable: "The kingdom of heaven is like yeast that a woman took and mixed into a large amount of flour until it worked all through the dough."*

2. Mark 4:3-20 – "³"*Listen! A farmer went out to sow his seed. ⁴As he was scattering the seed, some fell along the path, and the birds came and ate it up. ⁵Some fell on rocky places, where it did not have much soil. It sprang up quickly, because the soil was shallow. ⁶But when the sun came up, the plants were scorched, and they withered because they had no root. ⁷Other seed fell among thorns, which grew up and choked the plants, so that they did not bear grain. ⁸Still other seed fell on good soil. It came up, grew and produced a crop, multiplying thirty, sixty, or even a hundred times."*

⁹Then Jesus said, "He who has ears to hear, let him hear."

¹⁰When he was alone, the Twelve and the others around him asked him about the parables. ¹¹He told them, "The secret of the kingdom of God has been given to you. But to those on the outside everything is said in parables ¹²so that,
" 'they may be ever seeing but never perceiving, and ever hearing but never understanding; otherwise they might turn and be forgiven!'"

¹³Then Jesus said to them, "Don't you understand this parable? How then will you understand any parable? ¹⁴The farmer sows the word. ¹⁵Some people are like seed along the path, where the word is sown. As soon as they hear it, Satan comes and takes away the word that was sown in them. ¹⁶Others, like seed sown on rocky places, hear the word and at once receive it with joy. ¹⁷But since they have no root, they last only a short time. When trouble or persecution comes because of the word, they quickly fall away. ¹⁸Still others, like seed sown among thorns, hear the word;

¹⁹but the worries of this life, the deceitfulness of wealth and the desires for other things come in and choke the word, making it unfruitful. ²⁰Others, like seed sown on good soil, hear the word, accept it, and produce a crop—thirty, sixty or even a hundred times what was sown."

3. Luke 8:5-15 – *"⁵"A farmer went out to sow his seed. As he was scattering the seed, some fell along the path; it was trampled on, and the birds of the air ate it up. ⁶Some fell on rock, and when it came up, the plants withered because they had no moisture. ⁷Other seed fell among thorns, which grew up with it and choked the plants. ⁸Still other seed fell on good soil. It came up and yielded a crop, a hundred times more than was sown." When he said this, he called out,*

"He who has ears to hear, let him hear."

⁹His disciples asked him what this parable meant. ¹⁰He said, "The knowledge of the secrets of the kingdom of God has been given to you, but to others I speak in parables, so that,"

'though seeing, they may not see; though hearing, they may not understand.'

¹¹"This is the meaning of the parable: The seed is the word of God. ¹²Those along the path are the ones who hear, and then the devil comes and takes away the word from their hearts, so that they may not believe and be saved. ¹³Those on the rock are *the ones who receive the word with joy when they hear it, but they have no root. They believe for a while, but in the time of testing they fall away. ^{14}The seed that fell among thorns stands for those who hear, but as they go on their way they are choked by life's worries, riches and pleasures, and they do not mature. ^{15}But the seed on good soil stands for those with a noble and good heart, who hear the word, retain it, and by persevering produce a crop."*

4. Luke 13:20-21 – *"^{20}Again he asked, "What shall I compare the kingdom of God to? ^{21}It is like yeast that a woman took and mixed into a large amount of flour until it worked all through the dough."*

A Few Kingdom Sayings

1. Matthew 4:17 – *"^{17}From that time on Jesus began to preach, "Repent, for the kingdom of heaven is near." "*

2. Matthew 5:10, 20 – *"^{10}Blessed are those who are persecuted because of righteousness, for theirs is the kingdom of heaven. ^{20}For I tell you that unless your righteousness surpasses that of the Pharisees and the teachers of the law, you will certainly not enter the kingdom of heaven."*

3. Matthew 10:7 – *"^{7}As you go, preach this message: 'The kingdom of God is near.'"*

4. Matthew 21:31 – *"^{31}"Which of the two did what his father wanted?" "The first," they answered."*

5. Mark 9:35-37 – *"³⁵Sitting down, Jesus called the Twelve and said, "If anyone wants to be first, he must be the very last, and the servant of all." ³⁶He took a little child and had him stand among them. Taking him in his arms, he said to them, ³⁷"Whoever welcomes one of these little children in my name welcomes me; and whoever welcomes me does not welcome me but the one who sent me."*

6. Luke 9:62 – *"⁶²Jesus replied, "No one who puts his hand to the plow and looks back is fit for service in the kingdom of God."*

7. Luke 17:21 – *"²¹nor will people say, 'Here it is,' or 'There it is,' because the kingdom of God is within you."*

8. John 3:3 – *"³In reply Jesus declared, "I tell you the truth, no one can see the kingdom of God unless he is born again."*

You Will Never Be The Same Again, Fasting Your Way To A Kingdom Consciousness. Your New Beginning Is Waiting On You!

12
When I am Fasting, What About My Children?

> *I have food to eat that you know noting about.*
> *- Jesus (Jn. 4:32 NIV)*

Many parents have a problem with meal preparation and television time during times of fasting because of their children. They ask the question, "What do I do with my children during the time the adults are fasting?" My answer is quite simple, "teach them to fast as well". We have all read or heard one of the most quoted passages in the bible that deal with children, Proverbs 22:6, *"Train a child in the way he should go, and when he is old he will not turn from it."* The chapter deals mainly with finances, and without question we need to teach our children how to handle money, but we also need to teach them to fast. As a matter of fact, as we teach them the disciplines of fasting (and praying), we will be teaching them to put their flesh under control, in submission, and thereby, how to have money and not allow money to have you.

The question we should raise is this, "Why did God bless you with children, and what are you going to do with them, to show HIM your appreciation?" Creflo and Taffi Dollar has a chapter in their book, The Successful Family, called "Be Fruitful and Multiply", where they investigate God's purpose for children. Using Psalm 127:3 KJV, which says, *"³Lo, children are an inheritance of the LORD: and the fruit of the womb is his reward"*, they offer a two-fold meaning. They share the observation that children are an assignment and a reward and therefore need to be cherished by parents as a blessing from God; therefore, treated as such. They write, "As a parent, your job is to build up, train, invest in and shape them in preparation for their future. When they are finally ready to leave home, your children will be equipped to follow God and fulfill His will for their lives. How well they are able to do this is your presentation to Him. In other words, the strength of their character and walk with God will have much to do with your "final grade." Not only are children an assignment, they are an inheritance as well. An inheritance involves possession, much like an estate. It's something that is placed in another's care until the rightful owner comes back to claim it. Your children are your estate. They belong to God, but He's entrusted you to manage them for Him. He gave them to you to care for until He returns for them. That means your stewardship of them will be evaluated."[35]

If we believe the final words of the last sentence, that we will be evaluated, judged on our stewardship of our children, then we will never take lightly what we say to or around them. We will never take lightly what we watch, read, or listen to in our homes or vehicles while they quietly observe. It is in those tender infant years that they are being shaped by us. We are painting the portrait of what they should look like when they grow up. What they will ultimately look like we indeed must stand in court to be judged for. If as parents we

---

[35] Dr. Creflo A. Dollar and Taffi L. Dollar, *The Successful Family*, Creflo Dollar Ministries, Denver, CO, 2002, pg 184

had to stand trial once a year for how we modeled character before our children I wonder how many children would be wards of the state. Often we are disappointed in the way our children turn out. But if they could be honest with us about who they picked up their habits, demeanor, etc. from, without us being offended or shouting "How dare you?" it would surprise us. It is simple to see, they learn to be teens and adults by watching and emulating our behavior. As well, their eating habits will be formed by what we feed them and what they see us eat. Typically, many people live in hind-sight when rearing children. They wait until trouble arises, overweight attacks (or health issues), drinking problems, addictions, pornography issues, abuse issues surface, before they say, "I wish I had not done that in front of them." I cannot overemphasize how many children have been messed up by careless living adults, some who have even called themselves Christians?

One of today's tragic statistics is the high rising percentage of children who have diabetes. Much of it is related to America's carbohydrate crazy cravings. Parenting on the run is causing health issues in the lives of our future generations. Many of our families in America live off of fast foods for breakfast, lunch and dinner. Donuts, chips and soda pops are a favorite snack. Other countries which have allowed fast food restaurants in them are experiencing the rise of obesity and other weight related illnesses. In many of the inner cities the rise of child diabetes is staggering. Go in any of the corner stores and you see drinks that have no nutritional value that are sold very cheap. Wet is not always good. The new energy drinks are carbohydrate night mares. Some parents allow their children to drink them. They should be institutionalized.

We ran a child-care service at our ministry several years ago. Every morning, one of the families would exit the bus with soda pop in hand. It was their breakfast drink. When I saw it one morning, I told the child-care leader that I would personally like to have a word with the parents. In the mean time, no open soda pops would be allowed in the facility in the mornings. Yes, that is correct. We banned soda pop (in the morning). I would like to have banned it all day but I didn't think the staff could take it. I later discovered that two of the children from the family that stimulated the ban, were on medication, and all were having behavioral issues in school. I had one suggestion. Change their diet. While we did see some improvement in their behavior early in the morning, and in school, they could not experience drug free living and trouble free behavior because the parents were enablers. Every time I saw them at church they had soda pop or chips or candy. I never saw them with fruit or even juice. If parents do not change *their* habits, children have a difficult road to travel. The fog in many children's future has been created by their parents. They run right into health problems and behavioral problems often because of their parents. Once they begin to have these issues many of them do not have a clue how to change them. Their record in the school system follows them wherever they go and they are touted as a problem child. The tragedy is that some early changes in their eating habits could have changed their future troubles. Fasting would have made a difference. No child however is going to introduce this to their parents (unless that child goes to that kind of church without their parents). Of course we know this is not impossible, but highly unlikely.

If I had grown up fasting, praying, tithing, serving others (missions), there are many things in my life I would have avoided. While I think I had a better than average childhood education, social and moral, spiritually, there were areas in which if I could have learned more it would have helped me escape some pitfalls once I had my own decisions to make. While my parents were nowhere near alcoholics, nor abusers of any kind that I knew of, I was exposed to alcohol and tobacco in the home. They would never have given us any and forbid the use of it as teens, but it was a lure because I saw it and it appeared to be a stimulus for having fun and/or looking "cool". I admired my dad; he is one of my heroes. I used to watch him at home with their friends especially during parties. Particularly I noticed my Uncle Jim and Aunt Julie, who looked so elegant with a cigarette and a glass. I thought so much of it, that it made me desire to take my first drink as a youth (J&B Scotch) from an easily accessible kitchen (floor level) cabinet. Most of my parents' friends were all in church, so it was not abnormal to see these things as a part of life (even as a Christian).

Today, the landscape is much more dangerous. Internet, cable television, the heightened awareness and availability of drugs, the "alternative lifestyle" freedom campaign, assisted by television and even government, the lack of medias' regulating of video and audio (lewd language and dress), all add to today's home, being ground zero for disaster and/or self genocide. Can you see yet, why good parenting today is as critical as ever? Can you understand why I wrote this chapter on the importance of fasting, for parents and children?

Would you have made all the mistakes you have made, if you had learned at to fast and pray properly at an early age? Some things you decided you would do, were merely done out of rebellion. Fasting, would have at least challenged you to consider an alternative. It would have given you a governor, a restraining trigger in your mind. Something to jolt your memory to say, "Hold on, you know better." A consciousness about going too far, that says, "I know better, even if I am not doing better", because I see a standard. That standard is Jesus Christ who lives in me. Now, do I let Him sleep or wake Him up and live through me in this and every situation? Many church going people do not grow up in homes with a standard of righteousness. Fasting (God's way) will guide you in developing that standard for you and for your children. I grimace when I think of what could have happened to me had I not been wooed by the Spirit of God and then said YES. What my children become, will be a crown, or a continuous crying for me. Much of this, I will decide its outcome. Our job as parents is to sow the right seeds and expect the right harvest. The soil is the ground we will initially help cultivate, but later,

they will make the choices on what they receive. We then live in the expectation of, "...when they are old, they will not depart from it" (Proverbs 22:6). Do your job early. Plant, water, and let God give the increase.

When you fast, not if, but when, put your children on the fast with you. Explain to them what fasting is. Use it as a teaching time. Use Isaiah 58 as your model. Check on their behavior in school and at play. Take notice continuously on how they deal with their classmates? Teach them that there are sacrifices one has to make in life. Teach them to give up a television show or television for a day and read the bible to them or watch a bible video. Teach them to pray beyond "Now I lay me down to sleep, I pray the Lord my soul to keep..." If they are old enough and you are free enough, tell them what fasting has done in your life.

You will not hurt your children removing sweets, chips, sodas, beef, pork or fried foods from their diet. Discipline will produce a future friendly life. Don't let your children have to grow up breaking bad habits that you could have allowed them to avoid.

My Testimony

In our household, we made a decision to have our children to fast when we fast. Theirs is not as strict as ours (my wife's is not as strict as mine), but they fast nonetheless. My father has been challenged with a shut down pancreas since early in life. He often told me to watch my weight as a safe guard against diabetes. I have suffered from gout, been diagnosed and prescribed medication for high blood pressure (which I never took – Thank God for healing and wisdom). My wife and I both come from families which have histories of obesity, as well as one or two of the big killers: cancer; heart attack; or stroke. The fasted life is a no brainer for my children to have exposure to. They have never had beef or pork, because my wife and I do not eat it. We do not drink soda pop. We occasionally have cookies. We have cake for birthdays. We drink soy milk (after weaning ourselves off of regular, 2%, 1% and skim). We eat cooked, raw (and juiced) vegetables and fruit. Obviously, so too do our children. As a result, they are rarely congested, have no allergies and have plenty of energy (PLENTY).

Let me ask you a few questions. Could your children (grandchildren, nieces, nephews) be better off eating more vegetables? Drinking water? Reading more of the Word? Watching more educational things on television? Learning how to build character? Well why not have them fast too? They will learn to know that it is a part of life that they cannot afford to live without, if you teach them or train them up in that mindset.

Psalm 78: 5b-7(NASB), says, *"He commanded our fathers, that they should teach them to their children, that the generation to come might know, even the children yet to be born, that they may arise and tell them to their children, that they should put their confidence in God, and not forget the works of God, but keep His commandments."*

When we learn anything that enhances our commitment to the kingdom of God, it is our parental obligation to pass those things down to our children. We are called to pass the torch to the next generation as a runner in a relay race. They are our teammates and our goal is to win as a unit not just as individuals. My father used to tell me why he worked so hard. He used to say that he made up his mind as a young man graduating from high school at 16 years old, that he was going to go to college, get a good job and make sure his children had a better life than his. He was really saying that every generation should be better off than the last. It is up to every set of parents to make the commitment to position themselves to offer that life to their children. That kind of commitment should begin when the child is in the womb. "When the noted architect Frank Lloyd Wright was still in his mother's womb, she would pace in front of large, elegant pictures of architecture and describe these masterpieces to her unborn son. What impact are you leaving on your children even from their days in the womb and from their infancy?"

Every day you should remind your children of what they look like in the eyes of Christ. There are several ways to do that. One is by making positive confessions from the word of God. The following is a group of confessions that were compiled by Neil Anderson a seminary professor and counselor.

A Parting Promise

Your children will eventually see you as a better parent while you are fasting. They will get a chance to see you more. They will get an opportunity to spend weekly time with you, not around the schedule of your time with a newspaper or your favorite television show or hobby. They will see you develop patience with them. They will begin to see your heart for God and will grow up with an understanding of how they want their marriage and family to look like. They will see what the model mother and/or father that they should be and will be honored to become that parent.

Affirmations and Prayers Over Your Children and Grandchildren

Heavenly Father, in the Name of Jesus Christ, I owe you thanks and praise for what you have promised in Your Word concerning my children (grandchildren). I affirm now and decree that all of my children (grandchildren) shall be taught of the Lord and great shall be the peace of my children (grandchildren) according to Isaiah 54:13.

I thank You and praise you for the salvation of my children (grandchildren) and pray that they will love the Lord God with all their heart, with their soul , mind and all their strength, as they love their neighbor as themselves, according to Your Word in Deuteronomy 6:5, and Matthew 22:37-39.

According to Your Word in 2 Corinthians 5:21, my children (grandchildren) are the righteousness of God in Christ Jesus. I thank you that they are the head and not the tail as promised in Deuteronomy 28:13. He who began a good work in my children (grandchildren) will continue it until the days of Jesus Christ, as found in Philippians 1:6.

Heavenly Father I thank you that my children (grandchildren) honor their father and mother and therefore their days are long upon the earth. I bring them up in the admonition of the Lord as instructed in Ephesians 6:4.

According to your Word Lord I decree that my children act out of the love of Christ that is within them every day of their lives. They never act out of selfish ambition or conceit and that grace abounds so that they have all sufficiency in all good things. I thank You that they have abundance for every good work. (Philippians 2:3,4; 2 Corinthians 9:8).

I decree and declare that my children (grandchildren) have the wisdom of God because they have the mind of Christ. They have wisdom beyond their years. They have the Godly wisdom from ages past, this present age and ages to come. I decree that they have genius in their genes because they have the Fathers DNA in them. They are anointed for every school, community, work and play assignment. Angels are on guard to watch over them day and night.

I decree that my children Grandchildren) are blessed with heavens best. They are the healed and I help them protect their health by the Word of God. They are the prosperous and I help them protect their wealth by the Word of God. They love in a constant overflow of great things happening to them. Everything they put their hands too prospers.

I decree that they are soul winners and kingdom princes and princesses. They are prayer warriors and worshippers. They are intercessors wherever they are. I decree that when they walk in a room the atmosphere changes because they are so in tune with their heavenly Father. That according to Mark 16:15-17, they tread on serpents and scorpions, cast out demons, speak in their heavenly language and the enemy fears the power of God in them.

According to Your Word in 2 Peter 1: 3, 4, you have given my children (grandchildren) everything that pertains to life and godliness. They walk in love according to 1 Corinthians 13. According to Ephesians 4, they never let the sun go down on their wrath, they never allow bitterness pride or anger to rule them, and they speak the truth in love. Glory to God!

Confessions for Your Children

(You say one of them first. Then have your children repeat after you.)

I am God's child, born again of *the* incorruptible seed of the Word of God. (1Peter 1: 23)

I am a new creature in Christ. (2 Corinthians 5:17)

I am the temple of the Holy Spirit. (1Corinthians 6:19)

I Am blessed (Deuteronomy 28:2-12)

I am overtaken with blessings. (Deuteronomy 28: 2)

I am the head, not the tail, above not beneath. (Deuteronomy 28:13)

I am the apple of my Fathers eye. (Deuteronomy 32: 10)

I am holy and without blame before Him in love. (1Peter 1:16, Ephesians 1:4)

I am chosen and dearly loved by Christ. (Ephesians 1: 4)

I am accepted in the beloved. (Ephesians 1: 6)

I am righteous and holy. (Ephesians 4: 24)

I am a faithful follower of Christ. (Ephesians 5: 1)

I am strong in the Lord. (Ephesians 6:10)

I am dead to sin. (Romans 6:1, 11)

I am a joint heir with Christ. (Romans 6:13)

I am more that a conqueror. (Romans 8: 37)

I am qualified to share in His inheritance. (Colossians 1:12)

I am firmly rooted, built up, established in my faith and overflowing with thanksgiving.
(Colossians 2:7)

I am bought with a price. I am not my own. I belong to God. (1Corinthians 6: 19, 20)

I am being changed into His image. (2 Corinthians 3: 18)

I am an ambassador for Christ. (2 Corinthians 5: 20)

I am the righteousness of God in Christ Jesus. (2 Corinthians 5:21)

I am a chosen generation, a royal priesthood, a holy nation, a people of God's own possession to proclaim the excellence which is in Him. (1Peter 2: 9, 10)

I am healed by His stripes. (1Peter 2: 25)

I am no longer living for myself but God. (2Corinthians 5: 14, 15)

I am an overcomer because greater is He that is in me than He that is in the world. (1 John 4: 4)

I am pressing toward the mark of the high calling which is in Christ Jesus my Lord. (Philippians 3: 14)

I am always triumphing in Christ. (2 Corinthians 2: 14)

You are now ready for the new you. Follow the path and it will lead you to L.I.F.E. (Love, Integrity, Faith and Excellence). One more thing, thank you so much, for allowing me to be a part of your journey. It was an honor to serve you in this way.

Chapter 13 is a fasting testimony from a very dear friend and powerful woman of God, Susan McIntosh. Your story is the next one to write. So tell it as you grow in Christ through the "Fasted Life".

13
Testimony from a Saint: Shut up Stomach! Hello God!

> **Isaiah 58:6 (KJV)** [6]Is not this the fast that I have chosen? to loose the bands of wickedness, to undo the heavy burdens, and to let the oppressed go free, and that ye break every yoke?

In my twenties and thirties, I was blessed to meet a number of powerfully anointed men and women of God. A few were Corrie ten Boom, Brother Andrew (author of God's Smuggler), Rev. William Hartley (mentored by Smiths Wigglesworth), Rachel Saint (sister of martyred and J. Sidlow Baxter. Each of their faith walks impacted my own walk with God. Most of my education all the way through college was Christ-centered. My parents were grounded believers and prayer was very much a part of our home life. My husband was raised on the mission field. We have Godly heritage. However, when one of our grandchildren disappeared, I realized, the God I knew was not the miracle-working God. Yes, He was my Lord and Savior. Yes, my prayer life and daily devotional time was all good and probably a lot deeper than that of most people my age; however, never in all of my days had I heard a miracle testimony and my family needed a miracle. The problem facing us was huge.

One night I cried out to the Lord to teach me to pray. "Lord God, I know You must do miracles. Teach me how to pray and receive miracles. We need our grandson found." The next couple of days it was as though I had been connected to a spiritual satellite station. I had heard from God before by way of a knowing but now the Holy Spirit was nudging me and I was not sure I was comfortable with His new way of communicating with me because He was up close, closer than I had ever known God. For one, the Spirit began to ask me to do uncomfortable things. For instance, while crossing a grocery story parking lot one day I felt in my spirit the Lord saying, "Pick up the trash that is on the ground by your foot." I was indignant so I said under my breath, "I didn't throw it down." He said it again and continued to bother me until I finally quickly picked it up, hoping no one noticed. The trash pick up continued for a few days. I must admit, I was no pleased, but I obeyed.

Then in the middle of the night that same week, out of my sleep I was awakened to, "Get up and read the whole book of Esther." I was desperate enough to find our grandson that I obeyed God. I sat in the living room close to the lamp and read the entire book in that one sitting. The Holy Spirit came back in on me again and said in a knowing in my spirit, "I want you to fast for three days like Esther did for her people." I had never known anyone who fasted. My response was, "What is fasting! Is it going without food?" The answer came back, "Yes, for three days, no food." I argued, "But, I have low-blood sugar." "Let Me take care of that. You obey." So, in obedience, and by an enormous step of faith, for three days and nights I fasted. At first I had a headache and I grumbled. The Holy Spirit came in on me again and I sensed Him saying, "When you hear from Me as readily as you do from your stomach, then I can talk to you." When my stomach growled and said things like, "Excuse me, Susan, it is 9 o'clock and we haven't had breakfast yet!" I learned to quickly respond, "Shut up, stomach" and "Hello, God!" It was not long before my stomach's voice was overridden with the most awesome dialogue with God Himself.

Like Esther, I knew that somehow my act of obedience and dying to self was making a way for me to represent my family in an audience with this King I was coming to know better and better, the more I obeyed His Spirit. I had not bartered with God. Instead of fasting to get His attention, I was fasting because He asked me to come away with Him and to want His presence "more than my necessary food". The Lord showed me that I, like Queen Esther, was standing before the King of all kings on behalf of those I loved. God gave me a beautiful song I still use in ministry today. I asked the Lord one day, "Where is the gap? What do You mean by 'standing in the gap' on behalf of others in intercessory prayer?" He said, "The gap is God's Anointed Presence!" Oh, wow! Sometime later, well after the fast, the Holy Spirit directed me to Esther 8:8 and told me that my King was giving me new authority to use His Name in declaration and "no man could revote it". I came to realize that even in a crisis, I can choose to partner with the King and as I listen and follow His instructions, I can be a history maker instead of settling into the role of a victim of the enemy's plans to bring destruction to me and my household.

When the three-day fast started, the trash pick up alert stopped so it was not such a bad trade-off, praise the Lord! By the second day it was as though someone had cleared the heavens for me right over my head. God was <u>so</u> much closer. I found my formal prayers of "Dear Heavenly Father" were replaced with a dialogue with Him that continued off and on through the days and even in the night. Wow! I forgot about food. At the end of the three days I knew what it meant to be a friend of God's. We had become close.

Peace reigned in my life. Even in a time of uncertainty, an anchor of peace was in my soul. A few months went by and still no word about our grandchild but miraculously, my family began to receive phone calls from people who would relate to us what the Lord was showing them when they prayed for our family. It was tremendous. God was building a team of believers, an army. Two members of the "team" are former FBI agents who are Spirit-filled. Their professional, anointed knowledge and experience was incredibly helpful. The more I obeyed the Holy Spirit in the tutorial of prayer, the braver I became in God. It became so clear to me that God was in the equation and He was HUGE! I came to personal know El Shaddai—I was interacting with the Lord God ALL-mighty! He was beginning to feel so close I could almost physically grab onto Him. Freed from fear and despair, I anticipated and expected miracles. I know unbelievers and the more religious of my friends thought I had learned some new coping skill. No, God and I were partnering together and it was good. Then one day I heard the Lord say in my spirit, "Fast for forty days." I actually still had some protest left in me because my immediately response was, "I'll be gaunt!" "No," He said, "eat bread and you'll come to know I AM the Bread of Life. I am ALL you need, ever!"

So, for forty days, I ate some kind of bread at mealtime—cornbread, whole wheat, tortillas. Inside, I began to feel a strengthening in God growing supernaturally inside of me. Ephesians 3:14-21 describes exactly what was happening to me. My faith was soaring because I was experiencing God's closeness, His love. Understanding was opening the Heavens for me. I had a vision of a Jacob's ladder going right up out of my belly and it rested on His Throne. I knew I had God's ear and He had mine! The concern for the safety of our grandchild was being replaced by a knowing that God had our little one in the palm of His hand and He was orchestrating something awesome out of the mess the enemy had dealt us. I was being "strengthened mightily in the inner man by the Spirit" and I was becoming an encourager to my family members.

The last evening of the forty-day fast, we had a dinner party at our home. It just so happened that some of our friends were in town from different countries and the most convenient way to see them all was to have them over for a meal. I did not tell them I was fasting. Food meant nothing to me by that time so I carried on preparing a lovely dinner and I set a colorful table. Seated around the table were two Nigerians. One had nearly lost his life for the sake of the Gospel. He shared a fascinating story of God's intervention of his behalf. There were two women from Vietnam and one had actually died some years ago. She remained clinically dead for three days while visiting Heaven. She was miraculously resurrected and she shared this amazing testimony with all of us. It was a Kingdom of God evening. No one seemed to notice that I passed up all the good food and munched on my piece of cornbread. Later, after dinner, my husband walked all of our guests out to their cars while I cleaned up the kitchen. There was one piece of quiche left. It was nearly midnight. By this time I did not bother to even close my eyes to pray because God and I had a running conversation going most of the time. I looked at the last piece on the plate and said, "God, it is nearly midnight on the last day of the fast. May I have that piece." "Sure!" was His reply. Down I chomped as I heard Him say, "Will you fast for Lent?" "What the heck is Lent? That's a Catholic thing isn't it!" "Never mind what it is, will you fast for Lent." "Well," I thought, "how bad can it be?" So, I answered, "Yeah" and gladly gulped down the quiche. Kathryn, one of our Nigerian guests phoned a few moments later to thank me for the evening. I took the opportunity to say, "You were raised Catholic, right? So, what the heck is Lent?" She answered, "A forty day fast before Easter." "O, okay. So, when does it start?" She replied, "Tomorrow." I quickly finished our conversation and bid her, "Goodnight." I stood in the kitchen floor with my hands up in frustration and said, "This is a dirty deal. You knew Lent started tomorrow and You let me agree to fast for Lent <u>before</u> I even knew what it was!" I could almost see His face as He said softly, "Yes, but will you come with Me, I want to talk to You."

With tears in my eyes I replied, "Yes, Lord, I'll come." Then, still a questioning daughter I asked, "So, what are we eating THIS time, not more bread, please!" He answered, "I want you to eat <u>when</u> I tell you and <u>what</u> I tell you. It is about learning to <u>hear</u> My voice and <u>obey</u> Me." Gulp! However, trust me; the next forty days were incredible. I could give you some funny stories because occasionally it seemed like He had forgotten humans eat. Some days I mused a bit and He would say things like, "Okay, eat three large carrots raw." That particular time I ate one and put the other two back in the refrigerator only to have Him bug me until I pulled them out and with much grumbling, munched them down. It was about learning to obey, but, in addition, I did notice that He was putting nutrients back into my body. Funny thing, He never did say, "Chocolate cake or ice cream!"

On the final day, Easter Sunday, the phone rang and our son said, "Mom, I found him. He is in New Zealand. Here is the number. Be brief in talking to him and don't be surprised if they take the phone away from him." I rang the number, heard our little guy's precious voice just for a few moments. Yes, they took the phone away from him and hung it up. I had no sadness, only joy. My heart was forever anchored in a new proven assurance that "He who hath begun a good work…will perform it." I stood there at the kitchen counter with tears streaming down my face. They sprang not from a broken heart but from a River whose origin was from under the Throne of the personal, miracle working God who had become my new close Friend. It was He who was watching over our grandson and no one could hide the little one from God's presence and it was He who was right there beside me rejoicing with me. He said lovingly to me, "See, I knew where He was all that time…"

For nearly ten years after that I fasted every Wednesday and as my husband and I traveled the world and spoke, I recruited from the nations a couple thousand of prayer warriors. Hundreds of them caught the vision and fasted with me on Wednesdays. We met at Father's knee, in the G.A.P. (God's Anointed Presence) to intercede. The King not only raised His scepter to us, in time, He handed us scepters of authority to decree in His Name. Every Wednesday the Holy Spirit gave us a Scripture prayer focus and we "chewed" on the Word as we decreed its Truth over one another, our families, our nations, and current world events. We not only experienced many, many miracles, we came to know our prayer answering God on a personal, Friend to friend level. Hallelujah. I now understand fasting is not just about skipping meals; *it is progressing on into living a fasted life*. I guard my eye-gate, ear-gate, and heart-gate so I am not "filled up" by the world. I want to always be *hungry for and fed by the King*. Fasting is never a formula we follow to get leverage with God. It is so much more about clearing the way so can hear His voice. If the Holy Spirit impresses fasting on your heart, ask Him for specific details regarding what to eat or not to eat and when to eat. The Daniel fast was tailor-made for Daniel. God probably has a tailor-made one for you because you also are personally special to Him. Ask. Listen. Follow His instructions. It is all about brining us into a deeper, more satisfying relationship with Him. Oh, yeah, miracles happen but they are the bi-product of being in the presence of the King!

Addendum: What a Christian Looks Like

- An Encourager
- Anointed
- At peace
- Authentic
- Belief in the Triune God
- Blessed
- Caring
- Compassionate
- Consecrated
- Considerate
- Consistent
- Courageous
- Dependable
- Devoted
- Discernment
- Disciple of Christ
- Enthusiastic
- Eternally Secure
- Faithful
- Flexible
- Forgiven
- Forgivers
- Generous
- Genuine
- Giving
- Grateful
- Holy
- Honest
- Humble
- Integrity
- Joyful
- Kind
- Loving
- Long-Suffering
- Mature
- Moral Excellence
- Not a Sinner
- Obedient
- Patient
- Peaceful
- Peacemaker
- Perceptive
- Powerful
- Purity
- Pursues Excellence
- Righteous
- Self-Controlled
- Selflessness
- Servant
- Sincere
- Social
- Spiritually Gifted
- Stability during Trials
- Steady
- Tolerant
- Transformed
- Transparent
- Trustworthy
- Turns the other cheek
- Victorious
- Virtuous
- Warm
- Winners
- Wise
- Workers
- **Looks like Christ**

Bibliography

Anderson, Neil, *Victory Over The Darkness, Regal Books, Ventura, CA, 2000*

Bueno-Aguer, Lee, *Fast Your Way To Health*, Whitaker House, New Kensington, PA, 1991

Colbert, Don MD, *Toxic Relief*, Siloam, Lake Mary, FL, 2001

Dollar, Creflo A. and Dollar, Taffi L., *The Successful Family*, Creflo Dollar Ministries, Denver, CO, 2002

Edwards, Grant, *Swimming Lessons, How to Keep Christians Afloat in a Sinking World*, Specificity Publishing, Springfield, OH,

Ford, Leighton, *Transforming Leadership*, InterVarsity Press, Downers Grove, Il, 1991

Hemphill, Ken, Empowering *Kingdom Growth EKG The Heartbeat of God,* Broadman & Holman Publishers, Nashville, TN, 2004

Husband, Darryl F., *The Altared Life*, Lulu.Com, 2008

Jackson, Larry, *Guilt Free Living-* Frontliners Men's Ministries, Charlotte, NC, 2003

Joyner, Rick, *There Were Two Trees in the Garden*, Charlotte, NC, Morning Star Publications, 1984

Kallestad, Walter P., *Wake Up Your Dreams*, Zondervan Publishing House, Grand Rapids, MI, 1996

Kempis, Thomas A., *The Imitation of Christ*, Grand Rapids, MI, 1993

Koessler, John, *Names of the Believers*, Moody Press, Chicago, IL 1997

Malone, Henry, *Shadow Boxing*, Vision Life Publications, Irving TX, 1999

Martin, Glen and McIntosh, Gary, *The Issachar Factor*, Broadman & Holman Publishers, Nashville, TN, 1993

McIntosh, Susan, ACTS Foundation, Inc. (Acclaiming Christ Through Service) www.actsfoundation.org, Shut Up Stomach: Hello God, 2009

Monroe, Myles, *Rediscovering the Kingdom, Ancient Hope for Our 21st Century World*, Destiny Image, Shippensburg, PA, 2004,

Muller, Wayne, *Sabbath*, Bantham Books, New York, NY, 1999

Peck, M. Scott M.D., *The Road Less Traveled*, Simon & Schuster Inc., New York, NY, 1978

Pierce, Chuck, and Dickson, John. *The Worship Warrior*, Regal from Gospel Light, Ventura, CA, 2002

Prince, Derek, *Lucifer Exposed*, Whitaker House, New Kensington, PA, 2006

Russell, Rex, What *the Bible Says About Healthy Living*, Regal Books, Ventura CA, 1983

Sanford, John, *The Kingdom Within*, Harpers Row, San Francisco, CA, 1970, Rev 1987,

Savard, Liberty, Producing the Promise-Keys of the Kingdom Trilogy Series, Bridge-Logos Publishers, Gainesville, Fl, 1999

Sepulveda Art, *How to Live Life on Purpose*, Harrison House, Tulsa, OK, 2004

Wall, Bob, Solum, Robert S., Sobol, Mark R. , *The Visionary Leader*, Prima Publishing, Rocklin, CA, 1992

Warren, Rick, *The Purpose Driven Life*, Zondervan, Grand Rapids MI, 2002,

Zigler, Zig, See *You At The Top*, Pelican Publishing, Gretna, LA, 1977

Merriam-Webster Online Dictionary Merriam-Webster, Incorporated, 2005

The New Century Dictionary, Appleton Century Company, New York, NY, 1948

NIV Naves Topical Bible, Zondervan Publishing House, Grand Rapids MI, 1994

Vine's Complete Expository Dictionary of Old and New Testament Words, Thomas Nelson, Inc., Nashville, TN, 1984, 1996

About The Author

Bishop Darryl F. Husband, Sr. is the Senior Pastor of Mount Olivet Church and founder of Life More Abundant Ministries. Bishop Husband's philosophy "You Can Have What You Say," is a faith based ministry that crosses cultures to change lives. His heart is one of a father, helping pastors and churches reach their full potential. These changes will help God's people to exhibit habits of godliness in every area of their lives, leading to what is written in John 10:10 "I came that they may have life, and may have it more abundantly."

For more than 25 years he has served as Senior Pastor to the Mount Olivet Church, a multi-cultural congregation. Since becoming the Pastor, Bishop Husband has initiated and implemented many ministries, including L.I.F.E Church West and soon to be announced L.I.F.E Church South. His passion for training leaders is evident through our ever growing Mount Olivet Leadership Education Network (MOLTEN) Bible Institute and newly formed Church Leadership Training School.

Bishop Husband received his Bachelor's Degree from Illinois State University in Foreign Languages. He later matriculated at Virginia Union University where he earned his Master's Degree in Divinity at the Samuel D. Proctor School of Theology. He earned a Doctor of Ministry degree in 2004 from Virginia University of Lynchburg. Bishop Husband has also done doctoral studies at Boston University.

Bishop Husband has several spiritual connections. Bishop Husband and Co Pastor Sherrine Husband are connected and covered by Bishop Wellington Boone's Fellowship of International Church's. He and Co-Pastor Sherrine Husband are also affiliated with AIM Fellowship of with Bishop Ira and Dr. Bridgett Hilliard. Bishop Husband also serves the Full Gospel B C F International as the Southern-Atlantic Regional Director for the International Intercessory Prayer Ministry under Bishop William Murphy Jr. Bishop Paul S. Morton is the presiding Bishop.

Bishop Husband has a heart for people of different ethnic backgrounds and has traveled to many countries around the world doing leadership workshops and leading worship: India (Chennai, Nagaland, Mumbai) Brazil, Finland, Cuba, Ukraine, and Africa (Ghana, Benin, Cote d'Ivoire, and Cameroon).

He is the author of *"The Altared Life"*, *"Discovering The Winner Within*; *Daily Readings From Proverbs-For Building Character"*, and soon to be released in 2010, "Transitioning the Traditional Church", his doctoral work. Also pending is a life motivational book entitled, "Success Is the Plan God Has for You". Bishop Husband released his debut CD "Instrument of Praise" in 2006. He has just released his latest CD "I Was Made to Worship" and is already working on his third project.

Bishop Husband is married to the former Sherrine Charity, and they are the proud parents of Darryl Frederick Husband II, Gabriella Sherrine Agape Husband, Jason Oliver and two others the Lord gave, Daytriel McQuinn and Eric Elam.

Loving
Giving
Self-controlled
Peaceful
Smiling
Powerful
Wise
Courteous
Loving
Considerate
Smart
Zeal w/ Knowledge
Bold-
fearless

unassuming
humble
gentle
powerful
thoughtful
thankful
cheerful
obedient
pure
kind
Respectful
understanding
passion
courageous
Ready at all times

Like Jesus!